THE ART OF CELEBRATION

The Art of Celebration

PETER MUDFORD

FABER AND FABER
London & Boston

First published in 1979
by Faber and Faber Limited
3 Queen Square London WC1N 3AU
Printed in Great Britain by
Latimer Trend & Company Ltd Plymouth
All rights reserved

British Library Cataloguing in Publication Data

Mudford, Peter
The art of celebration.
1. European literature—19th century   2. European
literature—20th century   3. Social change
I. Title
809'.034   PN761

ISBN 0–571–10852–0

for
R.R.A.

Consequently I rejoice, having to construct something
Upon which to rejoice . . .

T. S. Eliot: *Ash Wednesday*

ACKNOWLEDGEMENTS

In the early stages of this work I was encouraged and helped by my supervisors at Oxford: Professor Nevill Coghill, Dr. J. I. M. Stewart and A. O. J. Cockshut. An early draft was read by Professor Geoffrey Tillotson, whose shrewd and sensitive judgement helped me, as it did his many friends and colleagues. More recently, the book has been much revised. Professor Barbara Hardy has made numerous suggestions and comments; and has been more than generous in her several readings of the work. Mr. Charles Monteith of Faber and Faber has given me invaluable assistance. Miss Valerie Elliott and, especially, Mrs. Barbara Brunswick have worked with great patience at the typing of several versions.

I am indebted to the following for permission to quote from the authors with whom this book is principally concerned: Leo Tolstoy: *A Confession, What I believe, What is Art?, On Life, The Kreutzer Sonata, The Death of Ivan Ilych* by permission of Oxford University Press; Leo Tolstoy: *Resurrection*, reprinted by permission of Penguin Books Ltd., © Rosemary Edmonds 1966; Thomas Hardy: Macmillan & Co.; Joseph Conrad: the Joseph Conrad Estate; Thomas Mann: *Stories of a Lifetime* and *Buddenbrooks*, Martin Secker and Warburg; Henrik Ibsen: translated by Michael Meyer, Eyre Methuen; Anton Chekov: *Lady with Lapdog, and other stories*, © David Magarshack, 1964; Chekov: *Plays*, © Elizaveta Fen, 1951, 1954, reprinted by permission of Penguin Books Ltd; E. M. Forster: *Where Angels Fear to Tread, The Longest Journey, A Room with a View, Howards End, A Passage to India*, Edward Arnold; *E. M. Forster, a life* by P. N. Furbank, Martin Secker and Warburg; C. Péguy: *Oeuvres Poétiques*, Editions Gallimard, Paris; G. B. Shaw: *Plays* by permission of The Society of Authors on behalf of the Bernard Shaw Estate; H. G. Wells: the Estate of H. G. Wells; R. Wagner: *The Ring* by permission of William Mann. Further details of all these books in copyright are to be found in the Notes to each chapter.

CONTENTS

INTRODUCTION

The purpose of art is to celebrate the human world we all share. In the twentieth century, with its absence of commonly shared convictions, and its accumulation of human catastrophes, the problem of believing (even in ourselves) and of continuing to find sources of hope has become increasingly difficult. The humorist may often seem to come closest to a solution: the world in his mirror is a joke; and taking ourselves lightly we may also be able to endure a little better, giving, at least, the impression of happiness. But we cannot rest there. The chimeras of purpose and significance rise up again; and with them the knowledge of how hard it is to find something upon which to rejoice. Here, the true artist serves as a 'persistent reminder of what men choose to forget': not by providing a form of escapism, but by imposing order upon chaos, and by reminding us of the values involved in individual life and human society.

In the course of the last hundred years, Man's knowledge of himself and of his universe has grown with enormous swiftness, not with any parallel increase in real self-knowledge (or so it would seem); this expansion has confronted him with an array of facts, hard to dispute or discount; and most of which serve to increase his scepticism about himself and his value. Art which is 'central to the consciousness of its time' has reflected this change; and has discovered in it a new kind of challenge.

In this book I intend to consider the period between 1860 and 1914, when these changes in belief about Man and his nature were beginning to make themselves felt; and to explore their reflection in the art of that time. In doing so I hope to achieve two things: first, to illustrate how an art of celebration continues to occur, even though Man's scepticism about himself and his world is becoming increasingly dark; and second, to modify the perspective in which the art of the late nineteenth century is commonly seen. The period is most often associated with aestheticism, decadence and disillusion. But in their very different ways, all the writers in this book accepted the harsh facts of existence, and still managed, through the power of their imaginations and the medium of their art, to construct something upon which to rejoice. Regarded from a European point of view, the art of the late nineteenth century remains one of the strongest testaments, not to decadence, but to the survival of the human spirit.

Without any doubt, the war of 1914–18 did much to change men's view of themselves and of the validity of their beliefs. It hastened a general acceptance of the idea that truth and falsehood were not eternal principles but relative judgements, however absolutely held by particular individuals. At the same time, it helped to destroy the idea of a European culture, permanent, purposive and progressive. In the words of Paul Valéry, 'l'oscillation du navire a été si forte que les lampes les mieux suspendues se sont à la fin renversées.'[1] Or as Aldous Huxley wittily put it in *Crome Yellow* (1921), the war had been a thorough holiday from all the decencies and sanities, all the common emotions: 'It was a step beyond Southend; it was Weston Super Mare; it was almost Ilfracombe.'[2]

But while the war played a very considerable part in speeding up the process of change, both social and individual, it worked upon forms of scepticism and misgiving that were already well established in the previous century. Increasing scientific knowledge about the natural universe, and of man's precarious eminence in the evolutionary scale, had produced what G. K. Chesterton has described as 'a curious cold air of emptiness'. The combination of an awareness that life involved a savage struggle for existence in which only the fittest survived, and a new dependence on what might be 'proved' as opposed to what might be accepted as true, either through divine revelation or imaginative assertion, inevitably came to affect the kind of art which men might feel it meaningful or true to create. It was no longer so easy to share Wordsworth's assurance in 'Tintern Abbey' of a 'sense sublime of something far more deeply interfused' in Nature and Man for human benefit. At the opposite extreme the vision of a scientific and materialist society, in which the arts would have no place, suggested the possibility of a dehumanised future. The best creative work of the late nineteenth and early twentieth centuries does not shirk or evade the particular challenge which a changing view of the universe brought about. In the work—as in the lives—of Thomas Hardy, Henrik Ibsen or George Bernard Shaw, the recognition of a harsh human reality is apparent; but more remarkable is their indomitable and imaginative spirit in the face of a destiny which appeared to many to have little to commend it. If there was in some of their attitudes a romantic heroism later to become unfashionable, there was also a dedication to the truth in their art, a will to endure, and a belief in the value of existence which still perhaps sets them in our eyes above their scientific contemporaries.

The forbearance in the face of fate of these nineteenth-century writers remains of relevance to our problems today. In spite of the terrors of the twentieth century little has changed. Undoubtedly, there is truth in what W. H. Auden wrote for Louis Macneice in his poem, 'The Cave of Making':

> . . . we shan't, not since Stalin and Hitler,
> Trust ourselves ever again: we know that, subjectively,
> All is possible.[3]

But a great deal of what we have learnt of ourselves, of our potential for cruelty, and of the world in which we live, was apparent to those who in the nineteenth century saw a 'Nature red in tooth and claw'. What has happened in our own times might even be seen—without too much exaggeration—as a terrible enactment of the world as Darwin had portrayed it, at least as that portrait was popularly understood. And that in turn created the kind of environment in which writers and artists had to find a new assurance and conviction.

The relationship between literature and belief is of a complex kind. In the novel and drama, the ability of the artist to create fictional characters and situations may focus attention on his psychological and social perceptiveness; in the presence of a great lyric talent, the feeling may involve the audience so deeply that any structure on which it is built may be forgotten. The dream of art works its magic upon us, and for the duration of the spell we are impervious to all else. To some, art may have only the purifying effect of a dream. But like the dream, it still bears the imprint of reality. In the presence not only of the individual work, but of the whole creative output of an important writer, the nature of the mark which life has left upon him, and the beliefs which at some level he holds about its nature is apparent.

It has now become a commonplace of our time that a writer's commitment has much to do with the value of what he writes; and this idea of commitment has for obvious reasons been most frequently associated with social and political convictions.

But these are only special instances of the problem of belief, which the imposition of form on the multiplicity and disorder of human experience has always involved. Walter de la Mare was among the first to express the problem in its modern form in his lecture on Rupert Brooke (1919): 'It cannot be too clearly recognised that the faith of a poet is expressed in *all* that he writes. He cannot either as a man or a poet live without faith and never does.'[4] The development of western civilisation since the mid-nineteenth century has not provided a kindly climate for this aspect of the creative life: a situation to which T. S. Eliot reacted like this in the year 1927:

> . . . I cannot see that poetry can ever be separated from something which I should call belief, and to which I cannot see any reason for refusing the name of belief, unless we are to reshuffle names altogether. . . . It takes application and a kind of genius to believe anything, and to believe *anything* (I do *not* mean merely to believe in some 'religion') will probably become more and more difficult as time goes on.[5]

In 1940, W. H. Auden, in an essay on 'Mimesis and Allegory', described what could happen to art if it became altogether separated from belief:

> Art is not metaphysics any more than it is conduct, and the artist is usually unwise to insist too directly in his art upon his beliefs; but without an adequate and conscious metaphysics in the background, art's imitation of life inevitably becomes, either a photostatic copy of the accidental details of life without pattern or significance, or a personal allegory of the artist's individual dementia, of interest primarily to the psychologist and the historian.[6]

The manner in which the writers of the late nineteenth century avoided these extremes remains an important aspect of their achievement.

Inevitably, a study of this kind has had to be selective. I have considered very little written after the First World War; and I have deliberately excluded D. H. Lawrence for this reason, although he might seem to have an obvious place in a book of this kind. If Lawrence had been included, W. B. Yeats and T. S. Eliot would have claimed a place, as would the later works of Thomas Mann. This would not only have made a cumbersome book, but obscured its intention to consider a culture in a state of transition between the massive achievements of the mid-nineteenth century—whether of Dickens, Balzac or Tolstoy—and the emergence of modernism. I have also, for more personal reasons, concentrated on works of drama and fiction, rather than poetry. In the period between 1860 and 1914—with the exception of Hopkins and Hardy—the most meaningful and challenging works seem to me non-poetic. Too often the poets reflect what was the central weakness of the age: an aestheticism which did not either in theory or practice justify itself. Finally, a study of this kind must leave out a great deal that would normally be of interest in critical appreciation. While trying to give sufficient attention to the 'art' of my title, I have still omitted much that might be said of technique and style, of form, and local excellence. What a work says can never be detached from how it says it; but the emphasis of this book falls more upon the symbolic than the formal qualities of works of art. In a sceptical age, the recognition of the problems implicit in belief, and the artist's solution of them, is one way at least of acknowledging his largest victory. The tact of art is needed to refresh our sense of what there is to celebrate; and the comprehensiveness of the artist's imagination to construct in an unassailable way 'something upon which to rejoice'.

Part One

In every period the Model of the Universe which is accepted by the great thinkers helps to provide what we may call the backcloth for the arts. . . .

C. S. Lewis: The Discarded Image (1964)

'THE BACKCLOTH CHANGES...'

Fundamental shifts in the way Man commonly regards himself, his relation to society, and to the universe in which he lives are often precipitated by the work of one outstanding individual: a Galileo, Newton, Darwin, Marx or Freud. But their work is equally the product of a long process of accretion—the result of forces which lie well outside the area of their own specialised interest. The shift in human attitudes which began to occur in the second half of the nineteenth century—notably under the influence of Charles Darwin—was also the product of forces at work for at least two centuries previously. Darwin's ideas served rather to crystallise conflicts that were already well established within the European consciousness; consequently, his ideas were rapidly assimilated, and achieved an authority that lay far beyond the scientific proofs supporting them. Darwin in fact acted as the final catalyst in the prolonged struggle between science and religion which originated in the great age of spiritual and humanistic belief in the seventeenth century.

The controversy over Darwin's influence still has not ceased. His ideas may be interpreted in such a way that they are not in conflict with Christian teaching; or they may be treated as the introduction to a biological account of human life, fundamentally incompatible with any religious or Christian account of things. In this chapter I am not concerned with the problems arising out of the interpretation of Darwin's ideas, nor with any attempt to assess the extent of his influence. By relating some well-known facts, I wish simply to illustrate the manner in which he brought to completion a change in attitudes towards Man and his place in Nature, which had been slowly transformed during the previous two centuries. Once Darwin had described and accounted for the evolutionary process, it became part of the context in which writers of the late nineteenth century grew up; and in its completeness as a model, which took no account of values, it created the need for a reassessment of values. In the later chapters of this book it will be seen how the attitudes of individual writers reflected the new scientific model; and how they worked in very different ways in their art to affirm the existence of values which might otherwise be lost sight of.

When Isaac Newton published his *Principia Mathematica* in 1687, he left no doubt in the reader's mind as to the ultimate significance for him of his life's work:

> This most beautiful system of the sun, planets, and comets could only proceed from the counsel and dominion of an Intelligent and powerful Being . . . to discourse of whom from the appearance of things does certainly belong to natural philosophy.[1]

Newton was by no means alone in his central conviction. When the Royal Society had been founded in 1667, its first President, Sir Thomas Sprat, had described the programme of the fellows as 'not to Meddle in Divine things' except for the purpose of displaying 'the admirable order and workmanship of God's universe'.[2] One of the greatest naturalists of the century, John Ray, showed his acceptance of this attitude to natural science in the title of his most famous work, *The wisdom of God, manifested in the works of the Creation* (1691). But even in Ray's work lies the origin of what later was to become a source of dispute. Describing his method in the 'Preface' to his work, Ray says that he has been careful 'to admit nothing for Matter of Fact or Experiment, but what is undoubtedly true'.[3] Nevertheless, the intention indicated by his title, and the theological beliefs which underlay it, inevitably affected his interpretation of the facts of natural history— in fact what he saw. His conviction of the wisdom of the Creator obscured from his sight facts at odds with his beliefs. Where there were defects they were attributable to Man:

> Man is always mending and altering his works; but Nature observes the same tenor, because her works are so perfect, that there is no place for amendments: nothing that can be reprehended.[4]

Man, for all his faults, is also a superior being, because no other creature in the sublunary world has been made to contemplate Heaven. This idea of natural philosophy as the study of the works of a wise and beneficent Creator, made possible by man's pre-eminent position in the 'great chain of being', formed an important tradition in the science of living things for the next one hundred and fifty years. To begin with, at least, it did not restrict or inhibit man's curiosity. A scientist-theologian, like William Derham, in the early eighteenth century, found the ubiquity of wise design exemplified in many fields, including cosmology, meteorology, geology, botany, zoology and human anatomy. Gilbert White, too, in his *Natural History and Antiquities of Selborne* (1789), demonstrated this interest in the goodness rather than the conflict within natural processes. His sharp eye observed in a clear-grained and knowledgeable way new instances of the 'wisdom of God in the Creation'.

But a few years after Gilbert White's *Selborne* was published, and in another country vicarage, Thomas Malthus completed the first version of *An Essay on the Principle of Population*, which was destined to challenge and finally shake the providential view of natural history. Ironically, the value which orthodox observers had attached to facts and figures also made it difficult to disregard Malthus's conclusions. Malthus had noticed that there was 'a constant tendency for all animated life to increase beyond the nourishment prepared for it';[5] and that while wars and disease helped to some extent to limit population, the consequences of overcoming these evils would be equally unpleasant. 'Gigantick inevitable famine stalks in the rear, and with one mighty blow, levels the population with the food of the world.'[6] Malthus dealt in a factual way with the statistics of population in a large number of countries, and with the possible remedies that might be used to prevent a future famine. As a priest of the Church of England he was also aware of the theological problem that his facts raised as to how a wise and beneficent Creator could create more beings than there was food for. He tried to get round this by supposing that pain had a salutary moral effect:

> It is the apparent object of the Creator to deter us from vice by the pains which accompany it, and lead us to virtue by the happiness that it produces. This object appears to our conceptions to be worthy of a benevolent Creator. The laws of Nature respecting population tend to promote this object.[7]

Malthus's justification was to prove less influential than his statistics. He had demonstrated convincingly that waste controlled the process of life; and it was this which, forty years later, led Darwin to formulate his theory of natural selection. When Darwin came to write his *Origin of Species*, fact also served to undermine the authority of those who were still inclined to the cheerful views of the earlier natural philosophers. William Paley, Archdeacon of Carlisle, for instance, had argued in his *Natural Theology* (1803) that the air, earth and water was teeming with delighted existence: 'A bee amongst the flowers in spring is one of the cheerfullest objects that can be looked upon. Its life appears to be all enjoyment.'[8] But Darwin, observing the same insect, wrote: 'Can we consider the sting of the bee as perfect, which, when used against many kinds of enemies, cannot be withdrawn, owing to the backward serratures, and thus inevitably causes the death of the insect by tearing out its viscera?'[9]

Even before Paley and Malthus wrote, however, there were plenty of signs that the old alliance between science and religion was breaking up; and that sooner or later people would be forced to decide which of the two presented a true 'model of the universe'. In one camp men believed that the Bible represented the truth given by God to Man, that the world was created, as Genesis told the story, in seven days—and according to Archbishop Ussher's calculation, in the year 4004 B.C. Milton expressed poetically this view of sudden and profuse creation:

> . . . The Earth obey'd, and strait
> Op'ning her fertil woomb, teemed at a birth
> Innumerous living Creatures, perfet formes
> Lim'd and full-grown . . .[10]

In the other camp, men started to believe what their eyes told them: that this could not be so. In 1795, a Scottish geologist, James Hutton, published his *Theory of the Earth*. He had first developed his ideas in an address to the Royal Society of Edinburgh, some ten years previously, but the publication of his book marked the first public attack on Archbishop Ussher's view of the age of the earth. Up until the time of Hutton, Noah's flood had been considered a sufficient explanation of the way in which fossils were distributed and geographical characteristics formed. But Hutton believed that a 'theory of the earth must depend on fact and observation.' Only an examination of the present construction of the earth could give us any information 'about the natural operations of time past.'[11] And what he observed around him was the action not of any flood, but of heat. Hutton's observations led him to his general theory of the earth's development: 'This earth, like the body of an animal, is wasted at the same time that it is repaired. It has a state of growth and augmentation; it has another state which is that of diminution and decay.'[12] Hutton also specifically contradicted the teaching of the Church in his observation that he could see 'no vestige of a beginning, no prospect of an end.'[13] Like Malthus, he attempted to reduce the impact of this by stressing the wisdom apparent in the Creation and, more particularly, in the human intellect. But he did

not succeed in assuaging the fears of his contemporaries, as Sir Charles
Lyell pointed out thirty-five years later in *The Principles of Geology*:

> A class of writers in France had been labouring industriously for
> many years, to diminish the influence of the clergy by sapping the
> foundations of the Christian faith, and their success, and the con-
> sequences of the Revolution, had alarmed the most resolute minds,
> while the imagination of the more timid was continually haunted
> by the dread of innovation, as by the phantom of some fearful
> dream.[14]

Lyell's emphasis upon the fears aroused by the French Revolution
when the truth of revealed religion appeared to be under attack was
correct; but conservative anxiety could not prevent the progress of
scientific research. If anything, controversy served to confirm and
publicise scientific theories, whatever their relation to the teaching of
the Church. Hutton himself died in 1797, but his work was continued
by John Playfair, who in 1802 published his *Illustrations of Hutton's
Theory of the Earth*. This provided even clearer visual evidence of what
Hutton had been saying about geological formations and their development. Inevitably, in time, a theory of geological development led to
questions being raised about fossils, and the evolution of life. Even
among men who had no desire to challenge the teaching of revealed
religion, more precise observation led to an accumulation of new fact,
and so in effect slowly shifted the area of dispute from the geological to
the human. This process can be seen in an interesting transitional stage
in the case of William Smith, a civil engineer who produced in 1815
the first stratigraphical map of England and Wales. He accepted
without any difficulty Hutton's theory of the deposition of the rocks,
which had recently caused such ill feeling; but he also made it clear in
his work on fossils, published two years later, that he regarded them as
special and divine creations which must have had their use in the mind
of the Great Creator. This process of slow erosion of formerly accepted
beliefs, like the separation of rocks from cliffs by the sea, was characteristic of the advance of scientific knowledge in the next half-century.
Charles Lyell in relation to the development of the earth, and Charles
Darwin in relation to the evolution of life, gave their theories a massive
authority through the steady accumulation of fact.

Lyell published the first volume of his *The Principles of Geology* in
the year 1830. Charles Darwin, whom it was later to influence profoundly, was then twenty-one. Lyell's theory of the continuous

development of the earth depended, like Hutton's, on 'limitless' time. He argued that modification in geography had been brought about by rivers, springs, seas, volcanoes, and earthquakes; and by material changes both within and above the earth. These natural processes, of which he gave many examples drawn from widely separated areas of the earth—North America, the Dordogne, Sicily, and the volcanic islands of the Chile seas—could only have occurred in innumerable millions of years. But although Lyell's views were incompatible with the teaching of the Church on the age of the earth, he took pains to make clear that his theory did not challenge any basic beliefs. Although the study of the earth revealed events which had occurred millions of years ago, and no sign of a beginning was apparent, yet there must have been a beginning somewhere. Man's appearance on earth, too, was relatively recent, and the first introduction of a moral and intellectual being remained a mystery as great as the creation of the planet itself. Although Lyell found plenty of evidence for gradation from one animal species to another, the case of Man appeared to him wholly distinct. The secrets of Creation were not to be mastered by the mind of Man:

> . . . To assume that the evidence of the beginning or end of so vast a scheme lies within the reach of our philosophical inquiries, or even our speculations, appears to us inconsistent with a just estimate of the relations which subsist between the finite powers of man and the attributes of an Infinite and Eternal Being.[15]

In spite of Lyell's determination to show the compatibility of his facts with much in Christian belief, his concept of limitless time and continuous development proved not only a scientific hypothesis of the first importance, but a turning-point in English intellectual history, because it established the authority of science in redefining a truth for the Church. Orthodox Christians were faced with the alternative of denying the truth of what Lyell said, or modifying their interpretation of Genesis, so that the seven days of Creation became a number of geological epochs. In this way the first part of a new model was established where not long before the idea of Biblical infallibility had been unassailed.

When Charles Darwin set out in his famous voyage of the *Beagle* in 1831, he took with him the first volume of Lyell's *Principles*, and he recorded that the book was of the 'highest service to me in many ways'. In particular, it was 'the wonderful superiority of Lyell's manner of treating geology' which impressed him. Most indispensable of all was the conviction which Lyell gave him of the time-scale of all processes on earth. In the *Origin* itself he was to record once more the particular nature of his debt:

A man must for years examine for himself great piles of superimposed strata, and watch the sea at work grinding down old rocks and making fresh sediments, before he can hope to comprehend anything of the lapse of time, the monuments of which we see around us.[16]

Without this concept of Time, Darwin's theory of evolution was also inconceivable.

Charles Darwin's *On the Origin of Species by means of Natural Selection, or the Preservation of Favoured Races in the Struggle for Life* was published on November 24, 1859. More than twenty-two years had passed since Darwin started his first notebook on evolution; his autobiography records the development of the theory in his mind. During the voyage of the *Beagle*, between 1831 and 1836, he had been impressed by three observations; and each of these had cast doubt on the idea of special and divine creations, as proposed in Genesis. First, he discovered in the pampas of South America great fossils covered with armour which bore a close resemblance to that on the existing, much smaller armadillos. Second, he noticed how animals closely related to one another replaced each other over the southern part of the continent. And third, he observed the similarity between the living things on the Galapagos Islands and in South America. All these observations pointed to some theory of the gradual modification of species; but he still lacked any hypothesis capable of explaining how the modifications occurred, or why there were innumerable cases of organisms beautifully adapted to their habits of life.

After returning to England he followed Lyell's example in geology by beginning a meticulous collection of facts which bore, 'in any way, on the variation of animals and plants under domestication and nature', in the hope that this might throw some light on the origin of species. He soon noted that men made use of selection in breeding the animals and plants which were useful to them; but he did not see the application of this principle to things in a state of nature, until he read Malthus on population in October 1838:

Being well prepared to appreciate the struggle for existence which everywhere goes on from long-continued observation of the habits of animals and plants, it at once struck me that under these circum-

stances favourable variations would tend to be preserved, and un-
favourable ones to be destroyed. The result of this would be the
formation of new species.[17]

Here was Darwin's working hypothesis; but so intent was he on finding
sufficient evidence to support it that it was not until he learnt of Alfred
Russell Wallace's identical theory that he prepared a paper for the
Linnaean Society, and eventually published the *Origin of Species*—
carefully avoiding the issue of the origin of Man.

But the *Origin* made enormous additions to the model. Whatever
the relation of Man, life had ceased to be a static, unitary thing, and
become a process of flow and development, in which an almost
inconceivable amount of waste had occurred over countless millions of
years. Whole species had been selected against, leaving only fossils or
bones as the signs of their once prolific existence. Here were no signs
of a kindly Providence, but of a vast, impersonal force which brought
about the extinction of those not favoured in the struggle for existence.
The law of natural selection was that those best equipped to survive
did so, and the rest (the majority) did not. When Man came to be fitted
into the model, as he shortly was, it raised questions not only about his
origin, but about his nature, his social relationships, and his ability to
believe that life was purposeful and significant.

The place of Man in the new model of the universe involved a more
fundamental shift in attitudes than is now easy to recall, when so much
has occurred to intensify scepticism about Man's motives and instincts.
Once he stood at the summit of the great chain of being, alone in
looking upward at the stars; the foundations on which he stood were
static, unchanging. If he was still conventionally regarded as the
quintessence of dust flawed by his own original sin, he was also to be
celebrated for the reasons which Hamlet once expressed: 'What a
piece of work is a man! how noble in reason! how infinite in faculty!
in form, in moving how express and admirable! in action how like an
angel! in apprehension how like a god! the beauty of the world! the
paragon of animals!...' Darwin determined in the *Origin* not to meddle
with so deeply embedded and finely wrought views, although he
privately admitted to Wallace that the question of Man seemed to him
the highest and most interesting problem for the naturalist. To avoid
stirring up public prejudice against his theory of evolution, he confined
himself to the hope that in future research light would be thrown on the
origin of Man and his history. This temerity was not shared by the man

who came to be known as 'Darwin's Bulldog', T. H. Huxley. A more
robust and aggressive intellect, Huxley took on himself the task of
communicating to as wide an audience as possible the new theory of
evolution, which became for him a crusade in the name of truth
against the literal-minded falsehood of the past. While Huxley
lectured up and down the country, often to audiences of working men,
the 'ape question' became yet another source of public—and this time
sometimes humorous—controversy.

> Am I satyr or man?
> Pray tell me who can,
>   And settle my place in the scale
> A man in ape's shape,
> An anthropoid ape,
>   Or a monkey deprived of its tail?[18]

But the issues were not only matter for verses in *Punch*. The question
of whether Man was in some way different from the rest of Nature,
either because he possessed a 'soul' (the mark of divine uniqueness at
work within him) or because of the faculty of reason and speech,
remained a troubling issue for many people. It was not helped by the
explorer du Chaillu, who went to Africa with the intention of finding
the ape which naturalists regarded as closest to man. At that time the
gorilla had scarcely ever been seen; and he made a sensational entrance,
which du Chaillu recorded: 'Nearly six feet high . . . with immense
body, huge chest, and great muscular arms, with fiercely glaring, large,
deep-grey eyes, and a hellish expression of face, which seemed to me
like some nightmare vision. . . .'[19] Du Chaillu then shot him, and firmly
rejected this apparition as being man's nearest animal ancestor·
    But once more fact was to prove sentiment wrong. The rejection
came from Huxley in 1863 in his *Evidence as to Man's Place in Nature*.
Using the strict scientific methods which he had learned from Lyell
and Darwin, amongst others, he produced in the second part of his
book an impressive anatomical analysis of the similarity between Man
and ape. Huxley's knowledge in this sphere began where du Chaillu's
speculations ended. His detailed comparisons led him to the conclusion
that the structural differences between Man and the highest ape were
great and significant; but they were not so impressive as those between
the highest ape and the lowest. So the process of development which
accounted for the evolution of other species could also explain the

origin of Man. Here, Darwin's theory of natural selection became
essential to Huxley; without it, his work would have remained a
contribution to comparative anatomy. With it, he was able to assert
that he saw no reason to suppose any interference in the process of
Nature in the production of all the phenomena of the universe from the
inorganic to the organic. To those (and there were many of them,
ranging from ordinary men in the street to philosophers like Carlyle,
who retorted: 'We are men and women, not a mere better sort of
apes') Huxley replied that the concern was irrelevant. Man's nobility
was not diminished by the knowledge that he was 'in substance and
structure one with the brutes; he alone possesses the marvellous endow-
ment of intelligible and rational speech, as well as the faculty for
storing and profiting by the knowledge of past generations.' By the
time that Darwin published *The Descent of Man* some eight years later
in 1871, his evolutionary views had achieved widespread acceptance
amongst the educated public. The development of life had taken place
over 'limitless time', with the evolution of new species occurring
as natural selection preserved those favoured in the struggle for existence,
and consigned the rest to extinction.

But the rapid acceptance of the new model, in its general outline,
would not have occurred, if the authority of the old had not also been
declining for quite different reasons. Oscar Wilde, in 'The Critic as
Artist', observed: 'The nineteenth century is a turning-point in
history, simply on account of the work of two men, Darwin and Renan,
the one the critic of the Book of Nature, the other the critic of the
Book of God.'[20] Renan, who himself rejected a career as the most
promising Catholic theologian in mid-nineteenth-century France to
pursue the new religion of Science, stands here for a movement that
deeply affected the beliefs of Europe by means of the 'higher criticism'
of the Bible. The challenge presented to belief in Genesis, by new
scientific facts, was being amplified by the work of theologians in a
movement pioneered by Reinhold Niebuhr in Germany at the
beginning of the century. In England the impact of this movement
made itself felt with the publication in 1846 of George Eliot's translation of Strauss's *Das Leben Jesu*. This work was concerned with the
discrepancies and improbabilities in the Gospel accounts of Christ's
life.

In time, it became increasingly clear that a struggle over the historical,
as well as the literal accuracy of the Bible would have to be fought; and

this manifested itself in the famous *Essays and Reviews*, published the year after the *Origin*. There, seven major theologians and scholars expressed the astonishing view that the rapid decline and disappearance of dogma was both inevitable and desirable. Religion was no longer to be regarded as something given by God to Man—particularly in the truth of Holy Scripture—but something made by, and for, man. Benjamin Jowett, the Master of Balliol College, Oxford, in his essay on 'The Interpretation of Scripture' asserted his belief that 'Christian truth is not dependent on the fixedness of modes of thought.' So dangerous were such views thought to be that two of the authors who were ordained were arraigned before the Ecclesiastical Court of Arches for expressing views inconsistent with the teaching of the Church of England. They were found guilty, and suspended from the ministry; but later, in an appeal to the Privy Council, acquitted.

Public quarrels of this sort began to make clear to the community at large that there were now 'two standards of judgement, the Bible and private opinion';[21] and this was the more significant in that it underlined the Church's inability to decide or impose what is believed, at a time when the *Origin*, by sheer force of facts, was establishing a view of the universe that was coherent, and relatively complete, without any reference to Christian teaching or theology. Huxley went so far as to concede that religious convictions which could not be proved might be true, but they were best left aside. Men could believe what they liked so long as it did not interfere with scientific truth. Meanwhile, science had created a model which touched on Man's behaviour, beliefs and values. In this respect it was capable of modifying his feelings, and altering his view not only of the world, but of the society in which he lived.

Before this long erosion of traditional belief had seriously begun, Dr. Johnson had written in *The Rambler*:

In this state of universal uncertainty, where a thousand dangers hover about us, and none can tell whether the good that he pursues is not evil in disguise, or whether the next step will lead him to safety or destruction, nothing can afford any rational tranquillity, but the conviction that, however we amuse ourselves with unideal sounds, nothing in reality is governed by chance, but the universe is under the personal superintendence of him who created it; that our being is in the hands of omnipotent goodness, by whom what appears to be casual is directed for ends ultimately kind and merciful;

and that nothing can finally hurt him who debars not himself from the divine favour.[22]

In the new model which science proposed everything appeared to be governed by chance, and the sense of kindly Providence had vanished. John Ray's view of Man, distinguished by the 'divine privilege' of his erect posture, his ability to perceive the beautiful and proportionable, the perfection of his body and senses, as well as his unique ability to contemplate the wisdom of God in the Creation, was destined to be rewritten by Wyndham Lewis in his sketch of twentieth-century Man:

> Turning his bloodshot eyes inward, as it were, one fine day, there he beheld with a start of horror and rage, his own proper mind sitting in state, and lording it over the rest of his being—spurning his stomach, planting his heel upon his sex, taking the hard work of the pumping heart as a matter of course. Also he saw it as a *mind with a past*: and he noticed with a grin of diabolical malice that the mind was in the habit of conveniently forgetting this *humble* (animal) and *criminal* past, and of behaving as though such a thing had never existed. It did not take him long to take it down a peg or two in that respect: The 'mind' . . . was soon squatting with a cross and snarling monkey and scratching itself.[23]

The major shift between Ray's and Lewis's view of Man began to occur when the 'backcloth for the arts' was changed by the new 'model of the universe' which Darwin, in spite of his diffidence, completed.

Nothing is more difficult to define with any accuracy than the spirit of an age. And even when we can see with some certainty the pervasive characteristics, the manner in which they are received and interpreted will vary from individual to individual. An age which appears sceptical may well be evangelical and revivalist for that very reason. But that 'melancholy, long withdrawing roar' of the sea of faith which Matthew Arnold heard so clearly in 1870 was not the murmur of a personal voice only; it pervaded the atmosphere in which the writers and artists of the late nineteenth century grew up. The strenuousness and difficulty with which Hopkins strives to preserve and defend his faith, the closely argued apology with which Newman defends his, are symptomatic of a threat not apparent in the spiritual distress of John Donne or George Herbert. Their inadequacies are personal: the result of human imperfection, and of sin. The believer of the late nineteenth century was compelled to struggle not only with himself, but against what he knew to be the attitudes (persuasive to many) of a Lecky, Huxley or Tyndall.

Loss of faith was not only a personal matter; but a question of knowing to which camp one belonged. The increasing authority of humanistic and secular minds was indicative of currents which were changing the nature of human society, and realigning the nature of individual relationships.

Wherever writers stood in relation to these changes, they inevitably exercised influence upon the formation of their personalities, both as men and artists. The materialist world which they confronted offered little consolation concerning the nature of human existence, while scepticism made assertion more difficult. The idea that 'nothing in particular is true', with its implied blurring of distinctions between moral and immoral actions, was taken by some as a new kind of integrity; and metaphysical despair found no obvious answer in any commonly shared convictions. Joseph Conrad portrayed this state of mind unequivocally in the character of Martin Decoud in the moments before his suicide: 'Both his intelligence and his passions were swallowed up easily in this great unbroken solitude of waiting without faith. His sadness was the sadness of the sceptical mind. He beheld the universe as a succession of incomprehensible images.'[24]

Some writers and artists, especially in the 1890s, succumbed like Decoud. The greater spirits not only survived, but triumphed. The following chapters will be concerned with the various forms of belief which they, as actors on 'the vast edges drear and naked shingles of the world' imaginatively asserted to resist the pressures of scepticism and despair; and in doing so gave new life to the art of celebration. (There were of course always those who remained true to the beliefs of Christian Europe; but with one exception they remain outside the scope of this book.) At the outset, we may recall what T. S. Eliot wrote of the scientific view of the past in the *Four Quartets*:

> It seems as one becomes older
> That the past has another pattern, and ceases to be a
>   mere sequence—
> Or even development: the latter a partial fallacy
> Encouraged by superficial notions of evolution . . .[25]

That other pattern of the past is the order of art itself.

B

THE CASE OF TOLSTOY

Doubt may be a manifestation of honesty; but it is not in the highest sense creative. To the important writer, though not to the lesser one, this poses a conflict between what it seems possible to assert, and what his imagination tells him he is trying to assert. The dilemma affects form and content alike. It can result, as W. B. Yeats knew, in a situation where 'the best lack all conviction and the worst/Are full of passionate intensity.' To avoid either of these extremes demands a particular form of tact—a combination of relevant attitudes with the aesthetic skill to integrate them in a work of art—which even the finest writers may not be able to achieve. Tolstoy in his late works suggestively illustrates the magnitude of the problem, falling short as he does of an effective integration of his beliefs with his art. He also helps to illuminate (and this will prove important for the rest of the book) how, though the changed context described in the previous chapter may influence the thought of a writer, the substance of his reaction remains of a deeply personal kind; and its value will depend on the 'inner harmony' which he succeeds in establishing with his audience. The influence of intellectual change is not, in the case of the writer, most interesting in its direct application, but in its more subtle effects upon psychological viewpoint, compelling him to represent the altered landscape in fresh metaphors, and to adjust, whether consciously or not, the perspective through which positive values are conveyed.

In 1879, Leo Tolstoy published his *Confession*, an account of a personal crisis through which he had been passing for the previous five years. *Anna Karenina* had been published in 1877, and *War and Peace* ten years before that. Tolstoy's reputation was enormous; and he had, as he said, everything which a man could wish for to make him happy: a wife whom he loved, and who loved him, a large family, ample money, and great fame. But what he came to perceive was the depth of his unhappiness; and the conclusions to which this led him continued to affect him, and what he wrote, until his death in 1910. His new-found convictions caused an increasing estrangement between him and his wife, making their lives together in later years almost intolerable, and leading to his death on a railway station, as he tried to escape from the life they had shared for forty-eight years.

Tolstoy's *Confession* is concerned with his prolonged struggle against suicide, which began when he was nearing fifty. Born in 1828, Tolstoy was baptised and brought up in the Orthodox Church. By the age of eighteen he had repudiated his faith; and from then until he was forty-five, he remained a man without belief. As far as his personal life in the army was concerned, he confessed: 'Lying, robbery, adultery of all kinds, drunkenness, violence, murder—there was no crime I did not commit, and in spite of that people praised my conduct and my contemporaries considered me to be a comparatively moral man.'[1] They also considered him the most outstanding young writer of his time. At thirty-four Tolstoy married; apart from the jealousies which tormented him and his wife in their remote life at Yasnaya Polanya, their life together created an emotional stability which enabled Tolstoy to do his finest work. But as time went on, Tolstoy found himself increasingly obsessed with questions he could not answer about the meaning and purpose of life. The intelligentsia had assimilated and accepted the teaching of contemporary science on evolution. Tolstoy could find no satisfaction in its vagueness: 'Everything evolves and I evolve with it; and why it is that I evolve with everything will be known some day.'[2]

One night Tolstoy was staying by himself in a provincial hotel at Arzamas; and there came to him then a sudden and terrifying vision of the inevitability of his own death. In the face of this fact, the problem of life's meaning: what is it for? what does it lead to? appeared to him answerable in only one way. The truth was that life in its arbitrariness and finality was meaningless. This conclusion tormented him increasingly: he found that he had to be 'cunning with himself' to avoid the opportunity for suicide. He had come to a precipice where he saw nothing ahead of him but destruction; he saw no purpose in his own existence (or that of others), ended, as it inevitably was, by death. And since life had lost its attraction for him, he saw no possibility of attracting others to life through art. Life was neither amusing, nor witty; it was cruel, stupid and senseless; a purposeless struggle in which death triumphed over all.

Wrestling with himself and these problems, Tolstoy turned to the

works of Socrates, Schopenhauer and Solomon, finding in them con-
firmation of what he felt that all was vanity, and death better than life.
In so bleak an account of things he recognised only one consolation:
'If I did not kill myself, it was due to some dim consciousness of the
invalidity of my thoughts.'[3]

Through his self-searching Tolstoy came to see the incompleteness of
rational knowledge. Irrational knowledge was faith which made it
possible to live: 'I began to understand that in the replies given by faith
is stored up the deepest human wisdom, and that I had no right to
deny them on the ground of reason, and that those answers are the
only ones which reply to life's question.'[4] He came to believe also that
he only lived at times when he believed in God, and that the one aim of
his life was to live in accord with His will. To do this, it was necessary
to renounce the pleasures of life, to labour, humble oneself, suffer and
be merciful. This led him in turn to regard the life of the ordinary
working people, and the peasants in particular, as the only real one: a
view which he was able to adopt because, as a landed aristocrat, he
lacked any personal experience of what it was like to live in poverty
and filth. Here lay the origin of his deep estrangement from his wife,
who saw in his giving up fiction for religious inquiry, in his desire to
rid himself of property and wealth, and his neglect of the material well-
being of his family, an act, at best, of moral irresponsibility.

Her protests and arguments, however, did not alter the course which
Tolstoy's life had now taken. The inner necessity which had enabled
him to write *War and Peace* compelled him with equal relentlessness to
pursue the vision which alone gave life meaning and purpose for him.
The Arzamas 'nightmare' was a deeply personal occurrence; but
Tolstoy's analysis of it, and of its effect upon him, is characteristic of
his time. It reflects, as great artists' crises may, a crisis of general import:
that many people found the new scientific and finite view of things
intolerable to live with, and felt compelled to find some means of
filling the void left by the lack of belief. Tolstoy attempted to supply
this in *What I Believe* (1884).

He related there how five years previously he had come to believe
in Christ's teaching; and at first sought to express this through participation in the rituals of the Church. But he could find little evidence in
the lives of the priests, or the attitudes of the Church as an arm of the
state, for what he saw as the truth of Christ's teaching. He also regarded
it as one of the most vulgar of all prejudices, expressed by the clever,

that it was possible to live without faith: the life-style of the wealthy and educated, now largely agnostic, provided enough evidence for this. He solved the dilemma by reverting to what he regarded as the fundamental truths of the Christian faith, which, if put into practice would change the nature of human life. Evil must not be resisted. If no one resisted evil, evil would cease to exist. The ordering of society, and the complex mechanisms of its institutions, were designed for the infliction of violence, both in the form of retribution meted out by courts of law, and through war. Human greed, lust and love of power, expressing themselves in various forms of violence, practised by individuals, institutions, and states upon one another, were the means by which people destroyed themselves. Man was 'lost in a snowstorm' from which the only escape lay in the renunciation of self for the service of others, and the welfare of the future. Adultery, violence, patriotism —any form of doing evil to others—had to be overcome, and this could only be achieved by returning good for evil.

These doctrines of non-violence, dispossession and simplicity of life were elaborated in his essay *On Life* (1887). By then his hostility to science had intensified. The view that 'the life of Man, as of any animal, consists in the struggle for the existence of his person, his race and his species . . .'[5] was the reverse of the truth. Human life consisted, or should do, in subjugating our animal personality to the law of reason for the attainment of good. Good meant striving for the good of others, which would result in the cessation of the fear of death, and of the thirst for pleasure. These goals were also realisable because the whole of life was not manifested in time and space: 'To believe in the destruction of life because the body is destroyed is the same as to believe that the disappearance of the shadow of an object when an object merges into full light is a proof of the destruction of the object itself.'[6] True human life is fulfilled outside space and time, and the love which exists there makes possible the attainment of the common good. So Tolstoy came to reconcile himself with the nightmare of Arzamas, and to formulate an answer to the prevailing views of science, as a means of healing a society that he saw to be sick. It remained for him to relate his new beliefs to the role of art in society, which he did in his essay *What is Art?* (1898).

'Art', he said, 'is a means of union among men, joining them together in the same feelings and indispensable for the life and progress towards well-being of individuals and humanity.'[7] The value of these feelings in relation to their goal is determined by their inclusion of 'the religious sense of the age', of which both artist and audience must be aware. Tolstoy defined this sense for his age as the knowledge that 'well-being for men consists in being united together.' Art, giving expression to this sense, would train men to experience those same feelings under similar circumstances in actual life. Art, without this religious sense, would not only be incapable of transmitting the highest feelings to which humanity has attained, but would simply pander to the educated and wealthy, appealing to their obsessions with social position, sexual desire and discontent with life. It would be impotent to encourage the growth of brotherhood, and love for humanity, on which the high claims of art alone rested.

Tolstoy's argument raises many questions—not least whether any evidence exists that art has ever modified actual behaviour. But he remains impressive in his desire for an art that celebrates a real good, as opposed to reflecting obsessions, either impoverished in themselves, or claustrophobically introspective, or both. But the harder problem arose, as Tolstoy himself discovered, not with the formulation of a theory of what art ought to do, but with its transcription into practice. Not only does the process of creation work through instinct and in-tuition, which cannot be controlled by theories of any sort; but also, because unbelief had become widespread, Tolstoy's convictions were inevitably a personal viewpoint which the majority of his readers found themselves unable to share.

Tolstoy's theories illustrate too the paradox of large and impressive human talents. By creating a special position for the people who possess them, they may in time come to divorce such people from a common human reality. The solutions which Tolstoy recommended for improving human life—notably his doctrine of non-resistance—remained those of someone who had managed to free himself from the responsibilities, conflicts and contracts which participation in a human world involves.

Tolstoy's power as a story-teller, his ability to give immediacy to persons and events had not declined; but the insistence on a particular viewpoint obstructed the fine and subtle investigation of personality, of feelings and ideas, which had characterised the earlier novels. *The Death of Ivan Ilych* opens as beguilingly as ever:

During an interval in the Melvínski trial in the large building of the Law Courts, the members and the public prosecutor met in Iván

Egórovich Shébek's private room, where the conversation turned on the celebrated Krasóvski case. . . .[8]

This actual trial turns out to be the frame for the much more important trial of Ivan Ilych's own life during a fatal disease. Tolstoy acts as prosecutor, revealing how badly Ivan Ilych has lived, in spite of his own good opinion of himself, which society has shared. As an examining magistrate, Ilych has quickly succumbed to a method of 'eliminating all considerations irrelevant to the legal aspect of the case', because this is expected of him. His brilliant marriage appeals to him because it is 'considered the right thing by the most highly placed of his associates'.[9] And when his wife's jealousy starts to displease him, he turns increasingly to his official life as a means of avoiding distress. Ilych aims in everything to make his life 'easy, pleasant and decorous'. Blind to the truth about his private life, and the corruption involved in his official duties, Ilych declines morally—a process which Tolstoy indicates in the details of his daily life: 'Sometimes he even had moments of absent-mindedness during the court sessions, and would consider whether he should have straight or curved cornices for his curtains.'[10] Appropriately, a bruise sustained while he is helping an upholsterer to 'arrange the drapes' marks the beginning of his illness.

Isolated by disease from his work and his family, he is compelled to come to terms with his mental and physical suffering, and to confront, as Tolstoy had at Arzamas, the idea of his own death. What he cannot understand at first is why he should suffer so much when he has lived so well; and only when he begins to perceive the emptiness of his existence, does he also succeed in freeing himself from the horror and pain of dying. As prosecutor, Tolstoy has emphasised the weaknesses to which Ilych has succumbed; and he has perceived them as an external observer. As a result, Ilych's final enlightenment does not seem artistically necessary. The reader does not participate in the change: he is informed that it has occurred. Inevitably, the effect of the tale falls short of that 'infection' of the reader's feelings at which Tolstoy aimed.

This imbalance between intention and means is again evident in *The Kreutzer Sonata*, and the long novel, *Resurrection*, though each in its own way is a considerable achievement. *The Kreutzer Sonata* uses a conversation between travellers on a train concerning contemporary marriage to introduce the main narration: Pozdnyshev's agonised account of how he came to murder his wife. Tolstoy fills the preamble with his own views on the hypocrisy and depravity which characterise the modern institution of marriage; and Pozdnyshev's tragedy is presented as the result of attitudes which society fosters, unaware of their corrupting power. In his youth Pozdnyshev has lived like others of his class, drunkenly, dissolutely, lecherously, while continuing to regard himself, as he has been taught, as normal, healthy and moral. When he does get married, he quickly discovers that the sexual attraction on which his relationship is founded provides no basis for harmony. Left alone, he and his wife have nothing to say to each other; and the quickly ensuing quarrels are only ended by a renewal of physical love. Tolstoy portrays the miseries of a marriage without sympathy or communication; but it lacks that inwardness of feeling which makes Anna Karenina's marriage real in its detail.

Only when Pozdnyshev's 'love' turns to violent jealousy—on the suspicion that his wife is having an affair with the violinist Trukhachévski —does Tolstoy begin to convey the violence of an emotion, and the horror of its effect. Like Shakespeare and Dostoievsky he is able to involve the reader in the feeling of committing a murder:

> I knew what I was doing every second . . . I knew I was doing an awful thing such as I had never done before . . . I realised the action with extraordinary clearness. I felt and remember the momentary resistance of the corset, and of something else, the plunging of the dagger into something soft . . .[11]

The effectiveness of the description, however, works against the intention of making Pozdnyshev representative of the ills of modern marriage. His tragedy is personal—the result of delusions and uncontrolled emotions. After the crime, he is struck by the insignificance of all that has offended him, and by the irrelevance of his jealousy. He concludes that if he had known all that he now knows, 'nothing would have induced me to marry her . . . I should not have married at all.'[12] But that too is a personal matter. The transformation of the actual world into nightmare through Pozdnyshev's frenzy remains more memorable than anything which he or Tolstoy has to say about marriage in a generalised way. In fact, such comments interfere with a narration which otherwise achieves an intense fervour.

In the two stories already considered, the pace of narrative prevents the extended intrusion of Tolstoy's personal views. But in the longer reaches of *Resurrection*, the flaws in Tolstoy's methods are strikingly apparent. Prince Nekhlyudov, the central character of the novel, is— like his creator—self-preoccupied to the degree that he lacks any sense of what other people are like. An aristocratic landlord who wants to give up his privileges and his property, Nekhlyudov also desires to atone to a servant girl he regards himself as having ruined. A young and innocent love had once existed between them; but after he joined the army, his life had become conventionally debauched, and she his victim. 'Then he had regarded his spiritual being as his real self; now his healthy virile animal self was the real I.'[13] He surrenders himself to a way of life which commands the world's approval, and stifles 'the voice in him which calls out for something different'. Nekhlyudov's decline is a matter for his own conscience; but the girl Maslova's seduction leads to her degradation and eventual arrest on suspicion of theft and murder. Nekhlyudov finds himself on the jury. Partly through his ineptitude, a miscarriage of justice occurs, and Maslova is condemned to go to Siberia. Nekhlyudov decides to atone by marrying her, and accompanying her on her journey.

This provides Tolstoy with the opportunity to depict the sacrifices Nekhlyudov is prepared to make for the woman he has wronged, and to explore the social conventions and injustices which permit her condemnation. His attempts to get Maslova's case reopened reveal to him how the law is operated by those with power and influence, in their own interests. and against those who have no means of defending themselves. Tolstoy had always disliked St. Petersburg; and here he had every opportunity to reveal how well grounded his prejudices were, by means of characters like the learned jurist Skovorodnikóv, and Senator Wolf:

> Wolf had just finished luncheon and in his customary manner was assisting his digestion by smoking a cigar and pacing up and down the room, when Nekhlyudov was shown in. Vladimir Vassilyevich Wolf really was *un homme très comme il faut*, and placed this attribute higher than any other.[14]

Tolstoy succeeds best in this novel when he allows character to reveal aspects of the corruption which he wants his readers to observe; and when he is writing about relationships—such as that between Nekhlyudov and his family—which he can describe from both sides.

But the central relationship between Nekhlyudov and Maslova cannot be accounted a success. Nekhlyudov's desire to atone for his guilt, to think well of himself once more, and to achieve forgiveness from Maslova, prevents him from even considering whether she has any desire to marry him, after all she has suffered. Unconsciously, perhaps, Tolstoy wrote into him some of his own new limitations, since he scarcely showed more understanding of why his wife did not share his views, and objected to his plans for destroying their family's prosperity. Maslova herself remains a shadowy figure in the novel, existing as the victim of society's wrongs, and the object of Nekhlyudov's hope of atonement. For all his views about society and the peasants, Tolstoy remained extremely restricted in the social range of characters he was able to portray. Nonetheless, the novel does achieve, in relation to the development of Nekhlyudov's character, a grandeur worthy of its name. In spite of his failings, his suffering extends the range of his pity and tenderness, arousing in him a love for his fellow human beings which he had previously lacked. But this does not mean, as Tolstoy hoped, that his outlook conveys itself to the reader as a solution to society's problems—or as a practical way of healing its corruption—not least because earlier in the novel Tolstoy has so effectively portrayed the intractable differences which arise from personality and perspective. The doctrine of non-violence to others will have no effect on those like Skovorodnikóv to whom, as a good Darwinian, 'all manifestations of abstract morality, or worse still, religious feeling are a despicable folly and personal affront.'[15]

Tolstoy did not altogether cease to write fiction without an obtrusive intention; and of his late works *Hadji Murad* at least deserves mention. The narrator is reminded by a thistle, which, though crushed by a cartwheel, still clings to life, of a man who had embodied a similar spirit of tenacity and courage. The fierce and free spirit of Murad attempting to save the lives of his family from his rival, Shamil, by making a dangerous political alliance with the Russians kindles Tolstoy's imagination. In this tale of border warfare and political intrigue he depicts the shaping of individual lives by events larger than they can control, or even know. Arbitrary, cruel and harsh as these events may be, they are incapable of destroying the finer qualities of men like Murad who have not been corrupted by the sophistication of Czarist Russia. When, at the close, Hadji Murad dies, isolated and surrounded by his enemies, he retains a savage splendour and humanity which Tolstoy has memorably depicted because he has left even Murad's fierceness and aggressiveness untouched by moral censure.

The artistic success of this tale serves to underline the magnitude of the task which Tolstoy had set himself in the definition of a new art, and in the works which attempted to exemplify it. Much in his critique of contemporary society has proved all too true in the course of the twentieth century. The year before his death Tolstoy wrote:

> It is our agitated life that is getting madder and madder, unhappier and unhappier, because men, instead of keeping to a spiritual, moral principle that would unite them in a society of peace and concord are guided by animal instincts. . . .[16]

In addition, the constraints necessary to keep order in society are necessarily becoming more violent, because men attempting to live without faith are guided only by self-interest. Tolstoy recognised how the authority of traditional beliefs had declined, and how impossible it was to live well without beliefs of some sort. His attempts to impose his beliefs on his art limited its effectiveness; it also illustrated how formidable a problem now confronted the artist in depicting a common human reality, without the beliefs underlying it appearing a merely personal testament. And conversely how, if he was not to continue to confine himself to 'local' events and persons, he had to find some way of seeing life whole in a society which no longer shared common assumptions.

Part Two: the face of Fate

The time seems near, if it has not actually arrived, when the chastened sublimity of a moor, a sea, or a mountain will be all of nature that is absolutely in keeping with the moods of the more thinking among mankind.

Thomas Hardy: *The Return of the Native* (1878)

3

THOMAS HARDY

Tolstoy's need to resist the cruel and meaningless interpretation of the universe which he read into evolutionary ideas was shared by many people. Some, like the hero of Mrs. Humphry Ward's *Robert Elsmere* (1888), attempted to create, as he did, a new Church out of the basic beliefs of Christianity; others, like Samuel Butler and George Bernard Shaw, tried to prove Charles Darwin wrong; and yet others again, like the members of the Rhymers Club, regarded beauty itself as an answer to scientific materialism. But the major writers achieved an affirmation implicit in what they wrote—in acts of imagination themselves. Recognising the dark account of things which scientific theory had erected, they nevertheless perceived in the quality of individual lives standards of possibility which stood against the prevailing sense of arbitrariness and emptiness. In confronting the Fate to which men now felt exposed, they also reasserted the presence of values which were not subdued by it.

Thomas Hardy read the *Origin of Species* as soon as it was published. He also read *Essays and Reviews*. Each made a vivid impression upon him, and he saw at once their significance for the time in which he was living. The grimness of the human situation which Hardy was to depict in his art may be compared to views expressed in the drama of the Greek tragedians; but more precise similarities exist between the picture of things which Darwin established as scientific truth, and the world as Hardy portrayed it in his novels: on the one side, the impersonality and callousness of the forces which operate through human existence, the waste of life, the power of chance; on the other, the absence of any kindly Providence, which might redress the balance of their effect upon us. Hardy's awareness of the new 'backcloth for the arts' is everywhere apparent; but his art assimilates and transcends it with a vision of a much higher order.

In an early novel, *A Pair of Blue Eyes* (1873), one passage memorably depicts the individual's insignificance in the evolutionary scale of things.

Knight, the central character, suffers a fall on the cliffs, and finds himself spreadeagled on a ledge. Unable to move, he has to wait until his lover, Elfride, returns with some means of rescuing him. In these moments of suspense, when any movement would cause his death, he begins to examine the surface of the cliffs in front of him:

> By one of those familiar conjunctions wherewith the inanimate world baits the mind of man when he pauses in moments of suspense, opposite Knight's eyes was an imbedded fossil, standing forth in low relief from the rocks. It was a creature with eyes. The eyes, dead and turned to stone, were even now regarding him. It was one of the early crustaceans called Trilobites. Separated by millions of years in their lives, Knight and this underling seemed to have met in their place of death . . . He was to be with the small in his death.[1]

The immensity of time, the vast multitude of extinct forms, highlight the insignificance of individual life, and the indifference of the process in which it is involved. More often, Hardy 'conveys' a sense of this through the events in particular lives, and the landscape against which they are set. In *The Woodlanders* (1887), for example, he characterises the forest like this:

> On older trees still than these huge lobes of fungi grew like lungs. Here, as everywhere, the Unfulfilled Intention, which makes life what it is, was as obvious as it could be among the depraved crowds of a city slum. The leaf was deformed, the curve was crippled, the taper was interrupted; the lichen ate the vigour of the stalk, and the ivy slowly strangled to death the promising sapling.[2]

Life is depicted here as an organic process in which the human and the natural bear the same deadly scars of the struggle for existence. Man, in spite of his intelligence, cannot escape from this process, as Henchard learns in the course of *The Mayor of Casterbridge* (1886):

> Externally there was nothing to hinder his making another start on the upward slope, and by his new lights achieving higher things than his soul in its half-formed state had been able to accomplish. But the ingenious machinery contributed by the Gods for reducing human possibilities of amelioration to a minimum—which arranges that wisdom to do shall come *pari passu* with the departure of zest for doing—stood in the way of all that.[3]

In Hardy's world all terrestrial conditions are intermittent, and the apparently fixed order of things at one moment has dissolved the next. As a novelist, Hardy is centrally concerned with the effect upon his characters of enduring in a world where this is the case. When Clym Yeobright in *The Return of the Native* (1878) gives up a lucrative career in diamonds with the intention of becoming a schoolmaster, Hardy comments: 'He had reached the stage in a young man's life when the grimness of the general situation first becomes clear; and the realisation of this causes ambition to halt awhile.'[4] Eustacia Vye, in the same novel —and for more emotional reasons—is portrayed as plumbing an abyss of desolation which leads to her premature death. Henchard, increasingly conscious of the void in which he is living, comes to look forward to the time when his suffering may be over; and Tess, the 'sport of the Gods', wants her happiness with Angel Clare to be brief, because she knows that in life it cannot last.

Hardy's perspective of the 'grimness of the general situation' changes from novel to novel; but it is never far from the centre of his attention. Human life must be endured on 'a blighted star'. In *The Woodlanders*, social snobbery and prejudice contribute a great deal to the sum of misery—though they do not account for it. Mr. Melbury thinks more of his future son-in-law's station than his heart, but he is scarcely to be blamed for the sorrows of her marriage to the well-born Edred Fitzpiers. Henchard is shown to be a proud, obstinate and jealous man; but he pays for his faults more heavily than he deserves. His jealousy becomes an instrument of the 'struggle for existence' which causes Farfrae to rise, and Henchard to fall. Here at once is one source of Hardy's greatness: the personal disaster is related to his view of the scheme of things, and his assessment of that scheme, as he sees it. Hardy's morbidity, and his dwelling upon grotesque incidents (for example, Angel Clare's dream-burial of Tess on their wedding night) are a not unnatural emotional outlet for an unflinching scrutiny of the human and natural world.

Hardy's organic vision imposes itself upon the detail of his novels, as well as their narrative as, for instance, in this passage from *The Mayor of Casterbridge*:

> The door was studded, and the key-stone of the arch was a mask. Originally, the mask had exhibited a comic leer, as could be discerned; but generations of Casterbridge boys had thrown stones at the mask, aiming at its open mouth; and the blows thereon had chipped off the lips and jaws as if they had been eaten away by disease.[5]

More importantly, it controls their tone. Even if human beings attempt

to overcome their weaknesses (as Tess does when she tries to tell Angel
Clare before their marriage of her seduction by Alec) malicious fate
says no; her letter never reaches him. When, finally, Angel desires
reconciliation, he arrives just too late to prevent her succumbing once
more to Alec for the sake of helping her brothers and sisters. Things do
not work out for people as they should. Whatever forces control
Nature force them to live out their lives in a scene as harsh as it is
desolate:

> Every leaf of the vegetable having been consumed, the whole field
> was in colour a desolate drab; it was a complexion without features,
> as if a face, from chin to brow, should be only an expanse of skin. The
> sky wore, in another colour, the same likeness; a white vacuity of
> countenance with the lineaments gone. So these two upper and
> nether visages confronted each other all day long, the white face
> looking down on the brown face, and the brown face looking up at
> the white face, without anything standing between them but the two
> girls crawling over the surface of the former like flies.[6]

Hardy's characters are surrounded by a Nature at best indifferent, and
at worst hostile; only the fittest survive 'in some sense' against the odds.
Hardy's greatness lies in his definition of that fitness, and the values
which redeem his fiction from mere depression and morbidity.

Some of Hardy's finest scenes occur on roadways; and behind the
particular scene stands the image of men and women as pilgrims and
wayfarers in the 'vale of soul-making'. In Chapter 40 of his earliest
major novel, *Far from the Madding Crowd* (1874), Fanny Robin, exhausted and abandoned by her lover, Sergeant Troy, attempts to make
her way by night to Casterbridge, where she will die. 'It is only by
seeing each movement along the road in terms of her goal that Fanny
can overcome her utter weariness: "Five or six steps to a yard—six
perhaps. I have to go seventeen hundred yards. A hundred times six,
six hundred. Seventeen times that. O pity me, Lord!" '[7] Now only
eight hundred yards separates her from the lights of the town which
represents a haven for the weary soul; but every method, stratagem, aid
seems to have failed her. Hopelessness comes at last. Then out of the
darkness a dog appears:

> . . . He was a huge, heavy and quiet creature standing darkly against
> the low horizon, and at least two feet higher than the present position
> of her eyes. Whether Newfoundland mastiff, bloodhound or what it
> was was impossible to say. He seemed to be too strange and

mysterious a nature to belong to any variety among those of popular nomenclature. Being thus assignable to no breed, he was the ideal embodiment of canine greatness—a generalisation from what was common to all. Night, in its sad, solemn and benevolent aspect, apart from its stealthy and cruel side, was personified in this form.[8] Fanny sees in the dog her last hope of persuading herself to go on; and while he moves in front of her, she follows behind. Between them a mysterious companionship is generated which itself renews Fanny: 'Whilst she sorrowed in her heart she cheered with her voice, and what was stranger than that the strong should need encouragement from the weak was that cheerfulness should be so well stimulated by such utter dejection.'[9]

With this strange companion, Fanny is enabled to reach her goal; and though the dog is stoned away by the man who drags Fanny into the poorhouse where she dies, Hardy indicates through this incident those guiding and restorative powers at work in Nature which make forbearance possible; but also lets us see through Fanny to a perseverance and hope of which she is both the embodiment and the symbol. The brutality and cruelty of life, and its inevitable ending in death, receive their just measure of attention in Hardy's fiction. But they are almost always touched and transcended by an emphasis more radiant and mysterious. The relationship between Fanny and the dog stands out as a memorable event in the course of the novel, while the end to which they both come is recorded as a matter of fact. As often in his work, the significance of the perseverance burns out the more brightly for the general darkness which surrounds it. On a larger scale, and at a different level, it is portrayed in the name and behaviour of Gabriel Oak, whose love for Bathsheba Everdene triumphs over vicissitude: 'Theirs was that substantial affection which arises (if any arises at all) when the two who are thrown together begin first by knowing the rougher sides of each other's character, and not the best till further on, the romance growing up in the interstices of a mass of hard prosaic reality.'[10] The endurance of Oak's love is depicted as larger and stronger than the normal passions and affections. This ability to survive, like that of the tree itself, makes it a force 'many waters cannot quench, nor the floods drown.' Fanny's purgatorial movement up the road and Oak's endurance in love complement each other as the physical and emotional expression of values that convey what is most memorable in Hardy's vision.

The Return of the Native was published four years later. In it Hardy used Egdon Heath as an organising setting. The structure and fabric of the novel is inconceivable without it, so that it acquires a significance equal to any of the central characters. The nature and quality of the place reflects something which Hardy perceived to be changing in the quality of life around him: its bleakness, austerity, inhospitability serves as a spiritual notation of people's inner lives, and the ill consequences which may ensue from that harshness—as they do in the case of Eustacia Vye, whose lonely figure is to be seen waiting for her lover at the outset of the novel. This view of Egdon's significance is put forward by Hardy in the first chapter of the book:

> The new Vale of Tempe may be a gaunt waste in Thule: human souls may find themselves in closer and closer harmony with external things wearing a sombreness distasteful to our race when it was young. The time seems near, if it has not actually arrived, when the chastened sublimity of a moor, a sea, or a mountain will be all of nature that is absolutely in keeping with the moods of the more thinking among mankind.[11]

He also regards it as a place concordant with man's nature: 'like man, slighted and enduring; and withal singularly colossal and mysterious in its swarthy monotony'.[12] The glimmering positive features established here at the outset remain an important aspect of the book's landscape.

The novel opens on a twilight afternoon in November, and ends just two and a half years later on a fine warm summer's afternoon with a breeze blowing. In that interval Hardy has portrayed the convulsive life of the heath folk, in the incidents of their individual lives, illuminated in their darker aspects by the fires which flash and burn over the heath. They shed light; they also purge, leading to the fairer weather of the book's end, and to the new illumination of the half-blinded Clym. Their symbolic role is plainly stated in the third chapter of the book when the bonfires burn up over the vast and sombre landscape with which Hardy is dealing:

> To light a fire is the instinctive and resistant act of man when, at the winter ingress, the curfew is sounded throughout Nature. It indicates a spontaneous, Promethean rebelliousness against the *fiat* that this re-current season shall bring foul times, cold, darkness, misery and death. Black chaos comes, and the fettered gods of the earth say, 'let there be light'.[13]

In the ensuing extremities the moral virtues and vices of those gathered into the circle of light will be revealed; the heath will put them through its own trial by fire. Wildeve himself admits that he suffers from the 'curse of inflammability' which has brought him down from engineering to inn-keeping, and will in the end bring about his own death by drowning. Eustacia lights bonfires as signals to bring her lover Wildeve to her. Described as the Queen of the Night, she herself embodies a destructive fire, with her pagan eyes, full of nocturnal mysteries: 'Assuming that the souls of men and women were visible essences, you could fancy the colour of Eustacia's soul to be flamelike. The sparks from it that rose into her dark pupils gave the same impression.' In her loneliness she longs for the 'abstraction called passionate love more than any particular lover'. This pagan and uncontrolled light in Eustacia lures herself and her lover, Wildeve, to their destruction.

But these dark fires find their positive contrast in the light which burns in Eustacia's husband, Clym. While her inner life seems to her a jail, his is a place of quite different feeling:

> As for his look, it was a natural cheerfulness striving against depression from without, and not quite succeeding. The look suggested isolation, but it revealed something more. As is usual with bright natures, the deity that lies ignominiously chained within an ephemeral human carcass shone out of him like a ray.[14]

But Clym is not unaware, as already indicated, of the grimness of the general human situation, and the fact that he almost loses his sight is both a comment on this, and on the strength of his inner illumination. Like Egdon itself, he is threatened with becoming a place 'exhaling darkness'. But he does not allow his affliction to master his spirit as it might have done. Even when he feels responsible for his own mother's death, and discovers his wife's culpability for what has happened, he remains unbroken.

In the very proximity of light to darkness throughout the book, Hardy does, however, suggest how close destructive force and creative energy lie to one another. As Eustacia abandons her husband, Hardy describes this ambiguity with the utmost force and subtlety. She is depicted for an instant 'as distinct as a figure in a phantasmagoria—a creature of light surrounded by an area of darkness; the moment passed, and she was absorbed in the night again.'[15] And again, as she goes to her death, it is with the night that she is identified; but night in which there still exists that pagan illumination belonging to moon-rob'd Astaroth:

They stood silently looking upon Eustacia who, as she lay there still in death, eclipsed all her living phases. Pallor did not include all the quality of her complexion, which seemed more than whiteness; it was almost light.[16]

After Eustacia's death by drowning, the atmosphere of Egdon is purified. Even the mysterious reddleman, Diggory Venn, has turned white by degrees; and Clym himself, after approaching despair, revives in his resolution to make himself an itinerant preacher. Like his earlier decision to become a schoolmaster, it reflects the survival of his love, and his continuing faith in the 'opinion and actions common to all good men'. It is not only the ability to endure, but the ability to endure with humanity that characterises the particular nature of Clym's triumph.

Hardy's view of life against the heath is founded upon a sombre sublimity: the path that leads to the light of the fine afternoon involves pain, death and sacrifice: within the night, there flickers the light which burns itself out, and the light which renews itself in spite of the dark, embodied in the twin figures of Eustacia Vye and Clym Yeobright. Here, the central greatness of Hardy's imagination reveals itself as the power to visualise enduring humanity against the background of a dark mythology. His power to celebrate life is achieved not by narrowing his scope, or averting his glance, but by confronting the dark and destructive forces which surround existence, and finding at the centre of human life an unquenchable resilience, fortitude and love. These twin forces of mythology and humanism are central to the structure and style of Hardy's novels. The mythology imparts to his manner a weightiness and grandeur which compels us to see individual lives in a larger context, while his investigation of humanity, depending as it does on the particular case, is invested with all the care and affection for the creation of the complete individual which is an indispensable part of any profound narration. His style and his structure, moving easily from the particular to the general, and the universal to the individual, encompass a complete vision of what existence is like, and so give to the particular values he celebrates an unanswerable force and conviction.

But while the mythology and the humanism recur in all Hardy's novels, except *Jude the Obscure*, the manner in which they are handled, the tone and emphasis undergoes a change in each one, so that the vision, in spite of the underlying pattern and coherence, is always conveyed as fresh and unique. The mythology of *The Woodlanders*, although once more closely involved with its setting—in this case the Hintock woods —is much less Olympian than in *The Return of the Native*. The characters most closely identified with the life of the trees—Giles Winterbourne and Marty South—are invested with a disinterested and enduring love, which is itself the product of their natural understanding and intuitive intelligence:

> They knew by a glance at a trunk if its heart was sound, or tainted with incipient decay; and by the state of its upper twigs the stratum that had been reached by its roots. The artifices of the seasons were seen by them from the conjuror's own point of view, and not from that of the spectator.[17]

In spite of their proximity to it, and also because of it, they both resist this incipient decay. Giles personifies an honesty, goodness, manliness and tenderness which endows him with 'a touch of real sublimity'. And though the love between him and Grace Melbury is thwarted, the unhappy events which stand in the way of its fulfilment do not detract from its quality:

> . . . It is not without stoical pride that he accepted the present trying conjuncture. There was one man on earth in whom she believed absolutely, and he was that man. That this crisis could end in nothing but sorrow was a view for a moment effaced by his triumphant thought of her trust in him; and the purity of the affection with which he responded to that trust rendered him more than proof against any frailty that besieged him in relation to her.[18]

Giles, the 'pure and perfect in heart', dies, possessed of a self-sacrificing love for Grace Melbury, which has the regenerative effect of 'banishing all sense of darkness from her mind'.

But the quality of goodness in Giles is magnified still further in Marty, the woodlander who, throughout Giles's life, has loved him unrecognised. By her detachment from the main action of the story— except in her protective love for Giles—Marty comes to symbolise an abstract human value:

> As this solitary and silent girl stood there in the moonlight, a straight slim figure, clothed in a plaitless gown, the contours of womanhood so undeveloped as to be scarcely perceptible in her, the marks of poverty and toil effaced by the misty hour, she touched sublimity at points, and looked almost like a being who had rejected with in-difference the attribute of sex for the loftier quality of abstract humanism.[19]

This abstract humanism is embodied in Marty's love for the dead man, and in her unshakeable sense that he was 'a good man and did good things'. Continuing love endows Marty herself with a quality comparable to that already described in Giles. In spite of the world's apparently callous disposal of human affections, and the variously destructive forces at work, some individuals remain as constant as the Hintock trees, while others, like Edred Fitzpiers and Grace Melbury, are capable of learning what love involves. As Hardy put it elsewhere: 'Love is faith, and faith, like a gathered flower, will live rootlessly on.'

It is, however, in *Tess of the D'Urbervilles* that Hardy's power to celebrate life, in spite of its harshness, assumes its most complex form. Even his style in this novel has undergone a sublimation, losing both the staginess of *The Return of the Native* and the somewhat ponderous magnificence of *The Mayor of Casterbridge*. Here Hardy writes with a clarity and conviction of unrivalled excellence. He gave the book the subtitle of 'A Pure Woman', and later defended himself against those critics who had complained of it: 'They ignore the meaning of the word in Nature, together with all aesthetic claims upon it, not to mention the spiritual interpretation afforded it by the finest side of their own Christianity.[20] He then referred to 'the great campaign of the heroine which begins after her seduction by D'Urberville'.

The survival of some kind of hope, in spite of the 'blighted star' to which Tess finds herself born, is central to Hardy's vision of his heroine. The hope is embodied both in Tess, and after her death in the surrogate for her, Liza-Lu. When we first see her with other girls at May-day revels in Marlott, Hardy describes them in the following way:

And as each and all of them were warmed without by the sun, so each had a private little sun for her soul to bask in; some dream, some affection, some hobby, at least some remote and distant hope which, though perhaps starving to nothing, still lived on, as hopes will.[21]

Much of Tess's tragedy derives from the false hope which her mother nourishes of re-establishing the family connection with the D'Urbervilles, through the attentions of Alec to Tess—even though he bears no relation to the original family. And while Tess does not seriously entertain Mrs Durbeyfield's matrimonial hopes for her, the idea is sufficient in itself to set the spring and snare the bird.

As with Clym Yeobright, Tess's misfortunes temporarily reduce her to a state in which she wishes she had never been born. The guilt of her sexual relationship with Alec bears in upon her a false distinction between herself and the Nature with which she had once felt identified: 'Walking among the sleeping birds in the hedges, watching the skipping rabbits on a moonlit walk, or standing under a pheasant-laden bough, she looked upon herself as a figure of Guilt intruding into the haunts of Innocence.'[22] Hardy points out that 'she is making a distinction where there was no difference', since Nature was quite as culpable as she. Furthermore, Hardy perceives in Tess another, finer quality not present in Nature at all: an ability to love that is unaffected by all she suffers, as for instance when she baptises her dying child:

> The kindly dimness of the weak candle abstracted from her form and features the little blemishes which sunlight might have revealed—the stubble scratches upon her wrists, and the weariness of her eyes—her high enthusiasm having a transfiguring effect upon the face which had been her undoing, showing it as a thing of immaculate beauty, with a touch of beauty which was almost regal.[23]

While abandoning those daydreams previously associated with D'Urberville, and determining to be simply the dairymaid Tess, she still regards her life as a pilgrimage in which she is trying to find a way of atoning for her guilt and the death of her illegitimate child.

Through her murder of Alec D'Urberville, Tess achieves at last a freedom with Clare unknown to her before. He has become the sacrifice to her guilt which is now stilled; the release from it brings about a kind of exultation. Tenderness also becomes dominant in Clare too. For six days at Bramshurst Court they find seclusion in an empty house, removed from the world of human and natural conflict. Outside Bramshurst, there is the pain of existence and inexorable fate; inside 'affection, union, error forgiven', which Tess values the more because she knows that its harmony can never be contaminated by the mutability of things, the rhythms of change which, as Hardy says elsewhere in the novel, 'alternate and persist in everything under the sky'. Tess's conviction enables her, when she wakes at Stonehenge to find that her trackers have come to arrest her, to bid farewell to Clare, not with a cry of defeat, but with a steady triumph: ' "I am ready," she said quietly.'[24]

The degree of Tess's triumph over Fate is felt fully only when remembered in the context of her rebuke to D'Urberville: 'O you have torn my life all to pieces.'[25] Neither that dismemberment nor the sport which the President of the Immortals has at Tess's expense over-comes her. Her good faith, and her ability to endure with a kind of happiness, survive. Angel too has changed: he has come to see that 'the beauty or ugliness of a character lay not only in its achievements, but in its aims and impulses. . . .'[26] Through Hardy's art, we too are able to see, with Clare, the beauty in Tess's nature.

But Hardy does not permit his vision of joy and reconciliation to end with his heroine's execution: its continuation as a perpetual possibility in the world is embodied, as though by a process of transference, in Tess's sister, Liza-Lu. Before Tess's arrest, she gives Liza to Angel Clare as the better part of herself who would have lived with him if Fate and D'Urberville had permitted:

> She is so good and simple and pure. O, Angel—I wish you would marry her if you lose me, as you will do shortly. O, if you would! . . . O I could share you with her willingly when we are spirits! If you would train her and teach her Angel, and bring her up for your own self! . . . She has all the best of me without the bad of me; and if she were to become yours it would almost seem as if death had not divided us.[27]

Immediately after the execution it is with this spiritualised image of Tess that Angel joins hands and goes on his way through life. As at the end of *Paradise Lost*, the tragic expulsion is associated with the advent of regeneration and renewal, made possible by a 'sacrifice'. Only an art that had continuously celebrated the goodness and loving-kindness in human life could have made plausible, within a few pages of Tess's capture at Stonehenge, Clare's departure with Liza-Lu. And the significance of this 'beauty born out of torture' is made all the more clear when we recall Hardy's attitude to the novel as embodying 'the views of life prevalent at the end of the nineteenth century'. Not only the pessimism was characteristic, but the victory which men of imagination still conceived of as possible.

Only in *Jude the Obscure* (1895)—the one novel of which the effect is depressing—does the sense of fortitude, endurance and ability to love become overshadowed by circumstance and event. Hardy's narrative skill, the depiction of individual lives crossing and recrossing in the complex skein of their development, is still just as assured. But the larger scope, the canvas against which such lives are seen, and with which they are involved, has faded away. There is little mythology in *Jude*, and the flattening of the landscape seems also to have had a restraining effect upon Hardy's view of character: the emphasis falls more upon its limitations and physicality than upon its splendour and sublimity. Arabella Donn is portrayed as so absolutely unlikeable that even her misfortunes arouse little sympathy. The grossness of her relationship with Jude, untouched by any feelings beyond self-interest, shows, by comparison with the depiction of relationships in the other novels, a coarsening of the artistry; and this applies too to other aspects of the novel's development.

The implausible introduction of Jude and Sue's children is wholly uncharacteristic of his finest work—not least because the incompleteness of their relationship has always appeared to derive from a sexual inhibition, which Hardy has chosen not to discuss openly. The children's deaths are also regarded in a more abstract and prophetic, than realistic manner:

> The doctor says there are such boys springing up among us—boys of a sort unknown in the last generation—the outcome of new views of life. They seem to see all its terrors before they are old enough to have staying power to resist them. He says it is the beginning of the coming universal wish not to live.[28]

Much in the new materialistic view of the universe, posing the question of purpose and meaning, pointed in this direction. But it had not been the emphasis of Hardy's earlier fiction. If he had continued to write novels, *Jude the Obscure* might have marked the beginning of a new period in which Hardy turned more to the territory of Ibsen's later plays. As it was, he recreated in his poetry an emphasis which both in its humanity and in its awareness of the general drama of pain had much in common with his earlier and more characteristic fiction.

At the end of *The Mayor of Casterbridge* Henchard's ageing has considerably lessened the spring of his stride, his state of hopelessness has weakened him and imparted to his shoulders, as weighted by his basket, a perceptible bend. His endurance, though, is not vanquished: 'My punishment is *not* greater than I can bear!' The following sentence crystallises much that is finest in the spirit of Hardy's fiction: 'He sternly subdued his anguish, shouldered his basket, and went on.'[29] Henchard's forbearance in the face of fate exemplifies courage and tenacity: values which, like loving-kindness and steadfastness, Hardy celebrates at the centre of the harshness of things. Sometimes they appear, as in *The Darkling Thrush*, as an almost inexplicable value:

> So little cause for carolings
>   Of such ecstatic sound
> Was written on terrestrial things
>   Afar or nigh around
> That I could think there trembled through
>   His happy good-night air
> Some blessed Hope, whereof he knew
>   And I was unaware.[30]

More often they are seen as aspects of the strength and appreciativeness of his own experience:

> Will these be always great things
>   Great things to me? . . .
> Let it befall that One will call,
>   'Soul I have need of thee':
> What then? Joy-jaunts, impassioned flings,
>   Love and its ecstasy,
> Will always have been great things,
>   Great things to me![31]

4

JOSEPH CONRAD

It was too cold for curiosity, and almost for hope. They could not
spare a moment or thought from the great mental occupation of
wishing to live. And the desire of life kept them alive, apathetic and
enduring, under the cruel persistence of wind and cold; while the be-
starred black dome of the sky revolved slowly above the ship, that
drifted, bearing their patience and their suffering, through the stormy
solitude of the sea.

Joseph Conrad: The Nigger of the Narcissus (1897)

Joseph Conrad differs as much from Thomas Hardy in his viewpoint
and vision of human life as might be expected from men whose
heredity, childhood and temperament had nothing in common. Hardy
was immersed for the greater part of his life in Dorset rural society: a
man of deep and passionate feeling which only found full expression in
his fiction. Conrad, after an unhappy childhood in Poland and Russia,
served until he was forty in the merchant marine, travelling widely in
the East—and with no intention of becoming a writer. Exiled, solitary,
aloof, Conrad lacked the finer grain of Hardy's humanity; and in fact
if we are to look for some similarity in temperament with other writers
of the period, it might be to Shaw that we should turn before Hardy.
To Shaw steering was a means of getting to Heaven; to Conrad steering
was the means by which man keeps chaos at bay. The man who steers
has at best a chance of surviving with some sense of moral identity in an
ordered community; at worst of losing his life, but achieving a kind of
victory in the unequal struggle with the powers that rule in a universe
just as pitiless as Hardy's. The individual's fight for survival (conceived
in many different ways) and its effect upon his moral identity lies at the
centre of Conrad's art, and of his achievement. As a stylist, his fiction
lacks Hardy's range of reference; and even when most assured, as in
Nostromo, his imaginary worlds for all their precision and detail are
grasping for something which they cannot quite reach. Conrad's
fictions achieve their stature by making an ordered narrative out of
experiences which he himself is uncertain how to interpret.

Joseph Conrad's first novel, *Almayer's Folly*, was published in 1895.

The dissatisfaction he had felt with the monotony of his life at sea erupted suddenly into the writing of fiction. Unsatisfactory though the novel is in certain respects—notably in the presentation of native characters—its central figure, Almayer, establishes a focal point for Conrad's world. Whether for reasons of language or temperament, Conrad was by no means so good as Hardy at the 'inscape' of character: his persons lack that luminousness which enables us to see through to their central qualities. Instead, the setting in which they are found reflects and amplifies, by suggestion, much that is true of their inner lives: and as with Hardy, much in that account is dark. But the landscape is not only metaphor; it also depicts the natural world, as this strikes a wanderer in the East:

> . . . plants shooting upward, entwined, interlaced in inextricable confusion, climbing madly and brutally over each other in the terrible silence of a desperate struggle towards the life-giving sunshine above—as if struck with sudden horror at the seething mass of corruption below, at the death and confusion from which they sprang.[1]

This brutal struggle for life has its counterpart in the character of Almayer, a decaying outcast in the river settlement of Sambir, living beside his unfinished and rotting folly. There he dreams of a treasure which would allow him and his half-caste daughter to live in a Europe he has never seen, and where his daughter's mixed blood would be overlooked for the sake of her beauty and his wealth. His fantasies originate in his association with the famous merchant adventurer, Tom Lingard: Lingard, who possessed great piles of shining guilders and a palatial mansion in Amsterdam, had once employed Almayer and persuaded him to marry his adopted Malaysian daughter. The Almayer whom we meet in the first chapter of the novel is described as contemplating the wreckage of his past in the dawn of new hopes. These hopes—based on the rediscovery of some of Lingard's lost fortune—rise from the decaying altar of the folly: a mansion on which he had spent what remained of his money in the belief that the British were about to colonise Sambir. The state of the folly suggests the values and beliefs which motivate Almayer; but it also reflects his inner life, where illusions of grandeur coexist with premonitions of complete despair.

Neither in the social picture nor in the personal portrait does Conrad's view lend itself to any optimistic account of things. In a vestigial way

Almayer still struggles to free himself from the savage life to which he feels himself reverting, and to which his wife has returned. But he only looks for reprieve by recapturing Lingard's lost treasure. Almayer's illusions serve to protect him a little from his isolation and solitude, when all the indicators point to their intensification, as well as to his corruption and decline. And his illusions are of course a part of that corruption, just as he himself is a part of the 'seething mass of corruption' in the jungle around him. When finally Almayer realises he must give up even his daughter to her lover, Dain Maroola, he reacts with all the harshness of one defeated in the world of his affections, as well as his material ambitions:

> And now his faith was gone, destroyed by her own hands; destroyed cruelly, treacherously in the dark; in the very moment of success. In the utter wreck of his affections and feelings, in the chaotic disorder of his thoughts, above the confused sensation of physical pain that wrapped him up in a sting as of a whiplash curling round him from his shoulders to his feet, only one idea remained clear and definite— not to forgive her; only one desire—to forget her.[2]

Almayer achieves his forgetfulness in his addiction to opium. The great and splendid rewards that he has envisaged for himself have wasted his energy, and caused the emptiness into which the structure of his life disappears, as the folly itself reverts to the jungle. The novel is permeated with a scepticism about existence which remains a central source of Conrad's artistic vision. But over and against this is the value which he attaches both to love and to moral endeavour, whether fulfilled or not, which remain to challenge what is destructive and base.

Conrad's scepticism also compels him to present moral endeavour not in the form of sentiments and aspirations which might have sounded well enough fifty years earlier; but as a much more ambiguous process involving recognition of the horror, and potential for evil that lies at the centre of human life. Marlow, in *The Heart of Darkness*, says his journey up the African river is like 'going to the centre of the earth'. On his way he is repeatedly confronted by evidence of human brutality and barbarism in a landscape equally savage: '. . . in and out of rivers, streams of death in life, whose banks were rotting into mud, whose waters thickened into slime, invaded the contorted mangroves that seemed to writhe at us in the extremity of an impotent despair'.[3] Life takes on the quality of nightmare; and like nightmare must be endured alone. The natives whom he sees abused, starved and done to death by their colonialist exploiters, becomes also an image of life at the earliest beginnings of the world—barbaric and disordered. The death of his steersman as he sails up river to find Kurtz, the ivory-dealer, is more than a practical disaster: it symbolises the need which Marlow acknowledges for something and someone to steer by in the abyss of human life.

And it is that abyss, into which Kurtz in his remote trading station, has most deeply fallen: allowing himself to be made a king of savages, and losing in the process the vestiges of humanity and civilisation. He has become 'hollow at the core', a 'soul without faith' existing in a void, with nothing either above or below him, in a condition of intense and hopeless despair. Marlow recognising this comes to see life as 'a mysterious argument of merciless logic for a futile purpose', paradoxically redeemed by another quality in Kurtz himself. Kurtz has 'something to say'; and it is this which has an enlarging effect upon Marlow's mind. In his savage kingdom, Kurtz has confronted things about himself which he did not previously know—and which remain unknown to those like his fiancée in England, who think only in terms of his nobility and greatness. His soul has gone mad with the knowledge; but in admitting the horror he has achieved a victory: 'It was an affirmation, a moral victory paid for by innumerable defeats, abominable terrors, by abominable satisfactions. But it was a victory.'[4] This victory, won at the heart of man's primitive and destructive impulses, at the very moment when moral degradation appears to have triumphed, enshrines the belief which Conrad opposes to his sombre view of existence. Conrad, like Hardy, perceives in human beings, a fundamental strength which, even if they appear, as in the case of Kurtz or Tess, to be overcome by their fate, retains something triumphant about it.

Something is the right word, because in spite of the authority of *The Heart of Darkness*, Conrad's judgment about the events he is describing often remains indecisive. He turns this to particular advantage in *Lord Jim*, where the various narrative viewpoints and the jumbled time-sequence are used to reflect Marlow's uncertainty about the central character. This alone gives to *Lord Jim* a particular originality in English fiction: Jim is not 'given'; the surfaces of his character emerge from the narrative. The desire to discover what happens to Jim is accompanied by the more serious task of trying to assess and fathom him.

When Jim abandons the pilgrim ship of the *Patna*, just a moment or two before he expects it to sink, he jumps into a well, an everlasting deep-hole, from which it will be his task to redeem some view of his moral identity. He is imperilled not only by this act alone, but by all the pressures exerted by his background and education when he falls short of the standards they have taught him to take for granted in himself. Conrad's artistry in making Jim's background and youth vivid in the early chapters of the book plays an important part in its over-all success, since it places Jim's leap in the context of a personality formed by conventional ideas that cannot be discarded without much pain; but which form in his case the flimsiest of defences, in a situation that is really testing.

Ironically, the villainous Gentleman Brown makes Jim into the gentleman he had failed to be. Brown represents that other side of human nature which Kurtz discovered, and which the romantic and idealist Jim had always tried to disregard: some 'obscure and awful attribute' just beneath the surface of human personality. But while Jim falls a victim to that destructiveness which he wants (and his public-school background had taught him) to disregard in his own nature, his death is still not seen as a senseless disaster in a tale of cruel and arbitrary events. He becomes by his sacrifice of his life an obscure conqueror of fame, with 'something exalted in his egotism'. He has remained faithful to his ideal of conduct, and so to his view of what life demands of a human being.

To Marlow there is always something shadowy in Jim's ideal: perhaps a wilful and purblind refusal to acknowledge the presence of a destructive element at work in the world; and yet a determination to save himself in spite of this. Marlow, the probing and reflective narrator, serves both to highlight the difficulty of evaluating Jim's character, and to stress the perspective which is characteristic of Conrad, as in his comment on the events which follow Jim's abandonment of the *Patna*: 'It was all threats, all a terrible effective feint, a sham from beginning to end, planned by the tremendous disdain of the Dark Powers whose real terrors, always on the verge of triumph, are per-petually foiled by the steadfastness of men.'[5]

So far I have concentrated on aspects of Conrad's fiction concerned with the individual, his inner life and conflicts, presented, as these often are, through the landscape in which he moves. But in much of Conrad's finest work, these conflicts are related to a wider social context, so that we see his particular form of belief in relation to the community at large, and recognise that his concern does not lie only with personal victory. To many people *Nostromo* (1903) represents Conrad's finest

C

achievement; it is certainly his most detailed and richly augmented. In the figure of the Capataz de Cargadores, Conrad depicted with a magnificent degree of integration those heroic and destructive qualities with which his imagination had always been preoccupied. The final paragraph in particular reflects the exhilaration and despair of Conrad's vision in a prose whose language and rhythm indicates too the complexity of a position not so far removed from Hardy's in *The Return of the Native*:

> It was another of Nostromo's triumphs, the greatest, the most enviable, the most sinister of them all. In that true cry of undying passion that seemed to ring aloud from Punta Mala to Azuera and away to the bright line of the horizon, overhung by a white cloud shining like a mass of solid silver, the genius of the magnificent Captain de Cargadores dominated the dark gulf containing his conquests of treasure and love.[6]

Here, at the end, Nostromo is seen to represent that resilient and ennobling aspect of the human spirit which exists as 'an unforgettable standard of perpetual possibility'. But the reference to the treasure even here echoes the ambiguity of the whole work, for it is the oppressively material concerns of the silver mine that have destroyed many people—particularly Charles Gould—in the Republic of Sulaco, both spiritually and physically. The horizon is fittingly 'overhung by a big white cloud shining like a mass of solid silver'. *Nostromo* is a novel which argues that the necessities of successful action often bring out the moral degradation of an idea good in itself. Charles Gould's direction of the silver mine, inherited from his father, is based on the notion that wealth is a means, not an end; and in this case to the improvement of the quality of life in Sulaco:

> Only let the material interests once get a firm footing, and they are bound to impose the conditions on which they alone can continue to exist. That's how your money-making is justified here in the face of lawlessness and disorder. It is justified because the security which it demands must be shared with an oppressed people. A better justice will come afterwards. That's your ray of hope.[7]

This view of the civilising effect of material well-being was one which Shaw had always advocated: poverty was an evil which had to be eradicated; but whereas Shaw used this as a basis for his philosophy of creative evolution, Conrad worked out in a profounder artistic way the more destructive and indirect effects of trying to implement it. Charles

Gould's service of a land 'waiting for the future, in a pathetic immobility of patience' results in his own destruction, and that of his wife. The ever increasing power that the mind exercises over him leads to the impoverishment of his feelings, relationships and humanity. No one realises this more clearly or suffers for it more deeply than Mrs. Gould:

> She saw the San Tomé mountain hanging over the Campo, over the whole land, feared, hated, wealthy; more soulless than any tyrant, more pitiless and autocratic than the worst Government; ready to crush innumerable lives in the expansion of its greatness. He did not see it. He could not see it. It was not his fault. He was perfect, perfect; but she would never have him to herself.[8]

The last of the Costaguana Goulds is to be consumed by the material interest of the mine; and her hope that there may be a successor is crushed also by the oppressive weight of the silver. Its fascination, and the greed, violence, war to which it leads does much to conceal the book's comprehensive pessimism, which rests in 'the immense in-difference of things'.

Gould's attempted defence of the 'commonest decencies of organised society' with the weapon of the mine is contrasted with Martin Decoud's boulevard levity in the face of what he sees as a tragic farce. He is destined to die from solitude and 'want of faith in himself and others':

> After three days of waiting for the sight of some human face, Decoud caught himself entertaining a doubt of his own individuality. It had merged into the world of cloud and water, of natural forces and forms of nature. In our activity alone do we find the sustaining illusion of an independent existence as against the whole scheme of things of which we form a helpless part . . .[9]

This is the more condemning a comment in that activity too is regarded as leading to its own particular ill ends, since activity in the novel, whether social or political, is directed towards 'material interest'. There is no other and sustaining belief which counterbalances the negative vision; rather it is complemented by Decoud's inability to interpret the world as anything more than 'a succession of incomprehensible images'. But again the richness and detail of Conrad's pigmentation tend to protect us from what is terrible in his vision: that, and the love which the magnificent Capataz de Cargadores inspires for his daring and courage, or the respect which Mrs. Gould creates for her steadfastness and lack of contamination by the obsessive power of materialism. Even

Nostromo himself becomes the hopeless slave of the San Tomé silver; and if in his personality Conrad offsets this with a romantic heroism, in Mrs. Gould, Conrad captures the deeper tones of a suffering humanity. While she possesses, by virtue of being Gould's wife, the advantage of detachment from immediately practical concerns, the lack of the 'most legitimate touch of materialism' in her character bears witness again to Conrad's implicit standard of possibility.

The sceptical despair of Martin Decoud does not lie at the centre of the vision from which Conrad's characters and novels take their being, although at times it comes close to being so, as in the final chapters of *The Secret Agent* (1907). The ability to love, and the heroism of Nostromo himself, are centrally highlighted by that dedicated articulation and structuring of the novel, which makes Sulaco so memorable a country to visit. Like the paintings of Delacroix, *Nostromo* is invested with a richness of detail and largeness of conception which gives colour and significance to its events. We come from it convinced of their importance, and of their bearing upon the human predicament. Unlike Hardy, Conrad does not achieve this by contrasting the general with the particular, but by turning the force of his moral scrutiny upon the particular, and perceiving within it a residual splendour. *Nostromo* amplifies the effect of the earlier *Lord Jim* by moving from the creation of an individual—complex as he is—to the creation of a complete society.

In *Victory* (1915) Conrad came closest to separating out the elements which had made his writing 'misty at the centre'. There he dwelt with no uncertainty upon the struggle within the universe between the forces of light and darkness, and saw in the indestructibility of love a force ultimately superior to those which threatened it. The novel was completed on May 29, 1914; and in a note to the first edition Conrad explained the reasoning behind his choice of title:

Victory was the last word I had written in peace time. It was the last literary thought which had occurred to me before the doors of the Temple of Janus flying open with a crash, shook the minds, the hearts, the conscience of men all over the world. Such coincidences should not be treated lightly. And made up my mind to let the word stand, in the same hopeful spirit in which some simple citizen of Old Rome would have 'accepted the Omen'.[10]

Victory is not, as this comment suggests, a realistic novel. The landscape of the island of Samburan represents for the lonely and sceptical

Heyst that other world in which he prefers to live, as a protest against the process of 'gorge and disgorge' in the great world outside. Heyst's own detachment owes a great deal to the influence of his Jove-like father, whose dying advice that he should 'look and say nothing' has encouraged a reflective scepticism. He is a man who finds in drifting a defence against life. Conrad describes him as a romantic, a gentleman, and one who at an early stage has done with facts. But the facts which Heyst is trying to live 'in spite of' stand out clearly enough. The novel is set in an age when men are described as 'camped like bewildered travellers in a garish, unrestful hotel . . .'. More specifically, the Company which first brings Heyst to the island, and then goes into liquidation, stands for the world to which he is understandably trying to find an alternative: the Tropical Belt Coal Company has left in the undergrowth only an image of waste and desolation. As in *Nostromo*, the forces of progressive capitalism are not seen to add to the sum of human happiness.

The novel, however, is also concerned with an immaterial kind of treasure in the form of the girl Lena with whom Heyst falls in love, and whom he rescues from the villainous hotel-keeper, Schomberg. He takes her back to the island; but the lovers are soon pursued by Schomberg's evil emissaries. The value of Heyst's relationship to Lena is contrasted with the destructive intentions of the three intruders from the outside world, who verify Heyst's contention that all action is bound to be harmful.

The three intruders are intent upon their own survival, whatever the cost to others; and they exist in a descending order of bestiality. At the top, ex-gentleman Jones embodies an evil, exhausted desire for authority. Hounded out of society, he carries with him its morbid and carnal appetites at their most sophisticated and dangerous. His secretary, Martin Ricardo, is the instrument of his boss's destructiveness: 'Ravish or kill—it was all one to him, as long as by the act he liberated the suffering soul of savagery repressed for so long.'[11] As Schomberg has previously noticed, Ricardo has the morals of a cat, a feral and instinctive savagery that admits none of the higher human instincts. Pedro, their mutual slave, is 'scarcely a man', with his enormous fangs and rolling, bear-like figure. The sullen, menacing hostility of the tropical forest finds its voice in him.

The effect of their invasion of the island on Heyst is to confirm his scepticism against participation, and to reinforce his belief in his secluded existence with Lena. Forced by their evil intentions to act, he discovers, in the final encounter with Jones, that his will had died of weariness. After the death of his tormenters and that of Lena, Heyst commits suicide. Or at least this is the implication of what Conrad writes. But Conrad does not describe the suicide because, as the title of the book suggests, he is concerned with something more important:

> The principal bungalow was blazing. The heat drove us back. The other two houses caught one after another like kindling-wood. There was no going beyond the shore-end of the jetty till the afternoon. . . .
>
> 'I suppose you are certain that Baron Heyst is dead?'
>
> 'He is—ashes . . . he and the girl together. I suppose he couldn't stand his thoughts before her dead body—and fire purifies everything . . . Let heaven look after what has been purified. The wind and the rain will take care of the ashes.'[12]

The purification by fire which absolves them from the evil of the human world is complemented by the manner in which Conrad portrays Lena's own death: 'The flush of rapture flooding her whole being broke out in a smile of innocent girlish happiness; and with that divine radiance on her lips she breathed her last, triumphant, seeking for his glance in the shades of death.'[13] But the intensity of this feeling also contrasts ironically with Heyst's own lament for his life: 'Woe to the man whose heart has not learned while young to hope, to love—and to put its trust in life.'[14] Heyst's scepticism had been in a large measure responsible for his sense of waste; but it also enables him to see the full value of Lena who provides the one great argument against his view that the world is a 'bad dog'. The fire which consumes them both burns away the scepticism and leaves the title a just comment on the value of their relationship.

Compared with *Nostromo*, *Victory* reveals a thinning in the density and profusion of the writing; but there is also a gain in the clarity of its viewpoint. The novel leaves no doubt that, though temporarily the forces of evil may appear to win, their victory is not sustained. The meanness and psychotic instability with which the intruders are conceived gives them an appropriate slightness in the scheme of things. Even Heyst's scepticism appears as a larger and more permanent threat than Jones and his assassins to the realisation of the potential good in human life. By fixing his novel on the extremes of the moral world, Conrad lost something in subtlety, but not in significance, proving once more that the deepest probing of existence nourished, rather than destroyed, his sense of the value of human life. One of his closest friends and admirers, Bertrand Russell, wrote in his essay on 'A Free Man's Worship' of 'victory in the struggle with the powers of darkness as the true baptism into the glorious company of heroes, the true initiation into the overmastering beauty of human existence'.[15] And, in doing so, he came close to defining the central quality of Conrad's art.

5

THOMAS MANN

Does not all one's love for one's fellow-men rest upon compassionate, fraternal recognition of the almost hopeless difficulties of his life? Indeed this feeling should be the basis of a kind of human patriotism. One loves one's fellow-men, because their lot is hard, and because one is oneself a man.

Quoted by Erika Mann in *The Last Year, a memoir of my father* (1958)

In a letter of the year 1906 Thomas Mann wrote: 'For men, heroism is an achievement "in spite of"; it is weakness overcome. . . .'[1] The works written before the First World War—*Buddenbrooks*, and some of the best of his novellas and stories—reflect this belief in two different ways. First, there is the conscious triumph of the works themselves: the artifact made perfect by skill, tact and discipline: austere attributes which nonetheless do not preclude tenderness, admiration and affection:

It won't do to call *Buddenbrooks* a 'destructive book' . . . 'critical' and 'sardonic'—that may be. But not destructive. It is too affirmatively artistic, too livingly graphic, at its core too cheerful. Must one write dithyrambs to establish oneself as an affirmer of life? Every good book that is written against life is actually tempting its readers on behalf of life.[2]

Second, the works recurrently include the figure of the artist, excluded from the comforting relationships of conventional life, and compelled to struggle in the face of fate, against weariness and disillusion, for the purpose of bringing his art to perfection. Like other men he must struggle too with passion and unreason. In the lives of ordinary men impulses such as these emerge in bizarre and morbid forms, which Mann depicts with irony and tenderness; like Wagner and Proust, he recognised how close we all live to the asylum. The artist only differs in that he possesses a gift for making these impulses the source of his art. Pathological—or neurasthenic—states circulate in the life-blood of what he creates; and disease itself becomes a central artistic preoccupation. The artist, in managing to overcome his disorder, achieves his particular form of triumph, and even in the stories where he does not appear we feel his presence in the modelled, plastic nature of Mann's style. His most ironic portrayals are reserved for those who ape the artist's calling and fail to live up to its immense demands, like Detrich Spinell in *Tristan*, and the narrator in *The Dilettante*.

The labour and painstaking care which had gone into the making of *Tess* or *Nostromo* became in Mann's case a theme within the created work: an image of man's victory against Fate. While we may surmise that Henchard's tenacity bears at some level the imprint of a comparable endeavour, Hardy's art (in the novel at least) is not self-preoccupied. Mann's fiction indicates a less practical, and less outward-looking, temperament: what we might describe as a metaphysical and philosophic Germanic spirit, immersed in the nature of things. But it would be crude to place too much emphasis on the difference in nationality, since the preoccupation of the artist with his work derives also from the loss of other external and absolute values. The aesthetic movement in England, like the symbolist movement in France, turned art into a cult. Mann rejected this, because he perceived in the artist-spirit an altogether sterner dedication, which had more in common with traditional religious discipline than with the veneration of objects practised by the aesthetes, or with the exclusive obscurantism of much in the work of the symbolists. The values demanded of the artist in his working life reflected those that were also necessary in the everyday world, threatened, as it was, by the decline of values.

Mann shared with Conrad a recognition that strength can only be achieved through immersion in the destructive element of personality. His early stories are preoccupied with the bizarre, morbid and sensational. Although these remained an essential part of the artist's experience—what von Aschenbach was to call 'exotic excesses of feeling'—they were transcended in the later works by sublimity of imagination which gave his fiction ampleness and stature. The groundwork was laid in the early stories which, although they are often decadent in theme, display a magisterial authority in moulding the material to the form: 'It was the nurse's fault. When they first suspected, Frau Consul Friedemann had spoken to her very gravely about the need of controlling her weakness. . . .'[3] The nurse's drinking results in the accident by which little Herr Friedemann, who gives the story its title, is deformed for life: 'He was not beautiful, little Johannes, as he crouched on his stool industriously cracking his nuts. In fact, he was a strange sight, with his pigeon-breast, humped back, and disproportionately long arms.' Johannes quickly discovers that his physical ugliness precludes him from love: 'Never again will I let myself in for any of it. To the others it brings joy and happiness, for me it can only mean sadness and pain. I am done with it. For me that is all over. Never again.'[4] With this decision made, Herr Friedemann achieves a kind of happiness, making his passion the theatre, where he has a regular seat in the first row of boxes at the opera house.

A new Commandant comes to the town with his beautiful, childless wife, Gerda von Rinnlingen; and from his first glimpse of her, little Herr Friedemann's composure is shaken. At each encounter his repressed passions shake his crippled being more fervently. The Commandant and wife inhabit an ordered world of outward beauty, which shows up the ugliness in that of Johannes. But this represents an inversion of the truth. Johannes is not without dignity and heroism in his struggle to deal with the problems of his deformity, while Gerda emerges as cruel and pitiless. She treats little Herr Friedemann with a patronising curiosity; and in the course of an evening party invites him to see her garden. The idealised scene evokes once more the contrast between beauty and ugliness:

> The scent of all the flower-beds rose into the wonderful, warm starry night. The garden lay in full moonlight and the guests were strolling up and down the white gravel paths, smoking and talking as they went. A group had gathered round the old fountain, where the much-loved old doctor was making them laugh by sailing paper-boats.[5]

When Gerda confesses her unhappiness to Johannes, he reciprocates by admitting his feelings for her:

> She did not repulse him, neither did she bend her face towards him. She sat erect, leaning a little away, and her close-set eyes, wherein the liquid shimmer of the water seemed to be mirrored, stared beyond him into space. Then she gave him an abrupt push, and uttered a short scornful laugh. She tore her hands from his burning fingers, clutched his arm, and flung him sideways upon the ground.[6]

His disgust with himself is more than he can bear; and little Herr Friedemann lets himself drown in the river.

Mann's controlled and ironic depiction of small-town society, with its snobberies and heartlessness, acts as a frame for a tale which, although it does not probe deeply (as Ibsen does in *Hedda Gabler*) into Gerda's personality, or that of her husband, is concerned with a precipitous imbalance in human character, and the destructiveness, whether of oneself or others, which is only just masked by manner and conventions. Like Wagner's Alberich, Johannes is excluded from love; he attempts to sublimate that aspect of his personality in the vicarious experience of the theatre. The story lacks sufficient weight to be moral; but its implications are serious, not least in their first soundings of the theme that art cannot substitute for life. A tale about physical ugliness, it is also anti-aesthetic.

Mann's early stories also show his developing range in the creation of character in various social environments. Whatever the setting, his eye focuses on some special twist in personality which isolates people from their fellow human beings. In *Tobias Mindernickel* he conceives a character who lives by himself at the top of a shabby and musty-smelling stair. In his elected loneliness, and gruffness, he becomes a figure of fun for the children who play in the street; but it is Minder-nickel who bandages the wound of a youth hurt in a street fight. The staunching of blood heals; but Mann suggests how the act also reveals a distortion in Mindernickel's affections. Tobias acquires a dog which arouses in him extremes of fury and tenderness. One day, wounding the dog accidentally, he nurses it with all the warmth of his repressed feelings. But once again the dog grows healthy again, and Tobias gloomy: 'Suddenly with a sort of frantic leap, he seized the animal, a large bright object gleamed in his hand—and then he flung Esau to the ground with a cut which ran from the right shoulder deep into the chest.'[7] Once again he tries to stop the flow of blood with his handkerchief, but the little dog dies: 'He laid his face against Esau's body and he wept bitter tears.'[8] Tobias remains a puzzle to the narrator, as he does a source of mockery to the neighbourhood, but through the repeated incident of the shedding of blood, which releases Tobias's compassion and tenderness, Mann indicates the involuted and pathological nature of his inner life.

As yet, Mann is working within a small compass, and developing his power as a depictor of the odds against which man has to struggle. *The Way to the Churchyard* stands out as a remarkable example of his ability to conceive this struggle in several dimensions. Praisegod's vice, like that of the nurse in *Little Herr Friedemann*, is drink; and on the way to the churchyard he furiously resents the figure of Life who passes him by on a bicycle. Like Friedemann and Mindernickel, Praisegod also has been expelled from normal social relationships. His wife has died six months earlier in childbirth. It was their third child, and born dead. The others are dead too, one of diptheria, the other of nothing in particular, save general insufficiency. And as though that were not enough, Praisegod has lost his job, 'been deprived with contumely of his position and his daily bread—naturally on account of his vice, which was stronger than Piepsam'.[9] His drunkenness has increased in proportion to his loneliness and isolation: 'When his wife and child were snatched from him, when he had...nothing to support him, when he stood alone on this earth, then his weakness took more and more the upper hand.'[10]

The final scene in Praisegod's life is played out on the path to the churchyard. The natural feelings, which found no outlet, suddenly erupt in a frenzy of rage and anguish. His anger at the cyclist who passed him becomes an obsessive rage against the world in which he lives. References to his own mode of life mingle with religious allusions and dissolute curses. His vision of the apocalypse brings judgment upon all those who stand gaping at him; but his fury is greater than his strength. Praisegod dies in the path where life has passed him by. In this story Mann succeeds in presenting as well as explaining Praisegod's disintegrating consciousness. He is like the figure we know on the streets who hurls curses as we pass; but like the cyclist he represents more than an individual life; he symbolises the outcast man, raising his fists against his fate but unable in the end to overcome or control it. Life itself is the disorder of which Praisegod becomes the victim.

All three stories are concerned with the relentless force of passion within the individual which breaks through his defences of reserve, or control. But the recurrent theme contrasts—and this is a major part of their originality—with the ironic detachment of their manner, and the restrained formality of their style. We feel behind them the reserve and discipline of the creative mind itself, imposing order on existence by a conscious act of will and self-restraint. Here is life, diseased by un-fulfilled passions and ending in death, they say; and here is art which by a conscious effort of will creates order and harmony out of life. Much more than in Hardy or Conrad, Mann's art is a self-conscious act, an assertion of health and sanity over disease and madness: a required triumph of formative mind over disordered existence. And the view of existence—for which Mann offers no other panacea—stands out the more clearly on that account.

The effect of these early stories is magisterial—but almost too bizarre. The ironic discipline is being stretched to its limits; and Mann was in danger of becoming an expressionist, concerned only with morbid conditions and involuted states. A lesser artist would have gone no further. But Mann now set out to place what remained a central aspect of his writing in a wider context: the decline of high bourgeois society in the middle years of the nineteenth century. *Buddenbrooks* was in part an autobiographical novel, a prolonged examination of his own origins in a family of wealthy and respected Lubeck merchants. Mann depicts them and their way of life in decline; but his emphasis does not rest upon decadence (as it might have done in the work of Wedekind or Hauptmann). Mann retained a patrician affection for his childhood environment, reflected in the loving and careful detail of the novel's massive development; and the decline is presented as an image of the processes at work in life itself, as much as the record of personal weakness. The ironist's art could not have encompassed the task without the aid of the chronicler's interest and involvement.

It would scarcely be true to say that *Buddenbrooks* celebrates a way of life; but the art is grounded in detached, careful and affectionate observation. The characters of the family, their friends and enemies become too familiar to permit of insistence upon any one feature of their decline to the exclusion of others. The picture is rounded, shored up with all the knowledge and experience which Mann can bring to its creation. As he himself asks: 'Isn't there a great deal of heroism in Thomas Buddenbrooks, worn out as he is, forcing himself to play his role?'[11] The answer is yes—but not in Thomas alone. It reverberates in the structure of the book, underlies it, and makes it possible:

> The boy may despise his home-town, when he storms off, impatient and without a qualm . . . And yet however much he may think he has left all that behind him, however much he may really do so, its deeply familiar image remains at the back of his mind or emerges from it in some bizarre way after years of oblivion. What once seemed ridiculous now becomes venerable. . . .[12]

Veneration is one part of the attitude which gives *Buddenbrooks* its stature: the loving care of the artist who ensures that all is right, whether his theme is decline or triumph. Mann pays the family the supreme tribute of thinking them worth the labour, the exactitude, the pains-taking development; and in doing so he also makes them an image of humanity, confronted with problems which are beyond their powers to control—but nonetheless continuing to struggle in their own way, until the end comes. No comprehensive vision of this sort moves

through Galsworthy's *The Forsyte Saga* (1921); and for this reason alone
it remains a far slighter fiction.

At the centre of the action in *Buddenbrooks* stands Thomas, merchant
and senator, whose life of practical involvement and earnest business
comes to a premature conclusion a little over the age of forty. By then
his major battles have been won, his future offers no obvious challenge,
or chance of promotion. Confronted by declining energy and little
further zest for what he has to do, Thomas faces the problem of man in
his isolation and self-doubt:

> His father had united with his hard practical sense a literal faith, a
> fanatic Bible Christianity, which his mother, in her later years, had
> adhered to as well; but to himself it had always been rather repellent.
> The worldly scepticism of his grandfather had been more nearly his
> own attitude. But the comfortable superficiality of old Johann could
> also not satisfy his metaphysical and spiritual needs; and he ended
> by finding in evolution the answer to all his questions about eternity
> and immortality. He said to himself that he had lived in his forbears
> and would live on in his descendants. And this line which he had
> taken coincided not only with his sense of family, his patrician self-
> consciousness, his ancestor-worship, as it were; it had also
> strengthened his ambitions and through them the whole course of
> his existence. But now, before the near and penetrating abyss of
> death it fell away; it was nothing, it gave him not one single hour of
> calm, of readiness for the end.[13]

Thomas realises too that in ultimate things there could be 'no help from
outside, no mediation, no absolution, no soothing-syrup, no panacea.'[14]
Nor can he find it in his only, and over-artistic son, in whom he had
once hoped to live on, renewed and strong. For a time Thomas seeks an
answer in philosophy; but in the end decides to leave spiritual matters to
God, and reserve his energy for earthly ones. He makes his will. Like
everything else in his well ordered life, even his marriage, the decision
is calculated, aimed at keeping disorder and inconvenience at bay. He
acts in the best traditions of the Buddenbrooks family; but as he himself has discovered, these have their limitations, even in the world of
practical affairs where the family's decline occurs. Life itself has taken
its toll both of convictions and fortunes; even the assiduous Thomas
can only attempt to hold in check the forces opposed to him. A
toothache and a poor extraction lead to his collapse in the street. For
the first time, the impeccably dressed figure is spattered with mud;

the order he has created succumbs to the disintegration of death, with neither practical nor metaphysical problems solved.

To Frau Permaneder, his sister, and the most vocal upholder of the Buddenbrooks name, it is vile and disgusting that the end should come like this. Her view betrays her lack of realism; but is not out of keeping with the respect shown for Thomas throughout the novel, especially in contrast to Christian, his brother. Aesthetic and feckless, Christian displays his contempt for the business community while living off its profits, and indulging his tastes for drink, women, and the theatre. Unlike many of his contemporaries, Mann did not see the aesthetic life as a necessary good. While Christian cannot endure the Buddenbrook way of life, he lacks the talent to prove himself anywhere else. Had Mann made him more sympathetic, he would have shown up to a greater degree the limitations of the hard-working and un-imaginative Thomas. But this was not his intention; for the values of stoic endurance which Thomas possesses have much in common with those which Mann regards as necessary for the artist.

The novel as a whole reflects Mann's description of himself as a man of balance; it is neither for nor against the way of life it records; but it treats the details of all the lives it includes with ironic affection and care. The decline of the family is not ascribed to any particular weakness or mistake; but to the accumulation of event and circumstance against them, as the current life moves away in another direction. Tony Buddenbrook would no doubt have had a happier life if she had married the young medical student she loved one summer at Travemünde. But the families of each regard the match as impossible. The Buddenbrooks, though not aristocracy, are absolutely separate from those struggling to enter the professional classes. But all that results from that rejection does the Buddenbrooks no good. Tony's marriage with a substantial dowry to a businessman who turns out to be in financial difficulties, and only to have married her for her money, does not in the end save her from ruin. Returning to her family with her child, she lives to contract a second and equally disastrous marriage (though with less unfortunate financial results), and see her only daughter married to Herr Weinschenk, who gets imprisoned for fraud. Tony continues to bewail the misfortunes of the family, and to resist in whatever way she can its decline; but to little effect. Thomas knows the world better than she: 'He had personally experienced the ruthless brutality of business life, and seen how all better, gentler and kindlier sentiments creep away and hide themselves before the one raw, naked, dominating instinct of self-preservation.'[15]

The shameless harshness of life fills him with revulsion and disgust; but it does not prevent him from going on; nor does it make him want anything different for his son. He wishes him to be a strong and practical-minded man, with definite impulses after power and conquest. These to the Buddenbrooks, and those amongst whom they move, are virtues. But Hanno, like Christian, though in a far more formidable way, does not fit the role. His gift for the piano, his early appreciation of Wagner, his ability to convey and be absorbed by emotion mark him out for a very different kind of future—or would do, if he had survived. In letting him die, Mann avoided a too obviously autobiographical and embarrassing comparison with his own talent and achievement, as well as a further opportunity to write down and slight by comparison what the Buddenbrooks stand for. In fact, as Thomas grows older, his stature grows through his increased self-awareness, and percipience about his own limitations. At Travemünde again with his sister, he recognises how once he would have preferred the mountains, but now could not endure their challenge: 'The eyes that rest on the wide ocean and are soothed by the sight of its waves rolling on for ever, mystically, relentlessly, are those that are already wearied by looking too deep into the solemn perplexities of life. . . .'[16] Thomas, in preferring the sea to the mountains, recognises his own weariness and illness; and surprises even his own sister by his powers of expression and feeling.

Around the Buddenbrooks themselves there exists a circle of associates to whom Mann also pays equally careful and respectful attention. They turn up at the family gatherings with their idiosyncrasies unchanged, suggesting a permanence which the book in its overall conception shows to be illusory. Some, like Jean Jacques Hoffstede, disappear in the course of the action; their places are taken by others. Only at the close when Gerda, Thomas's widow, decides to return to Amsterdam does the Buddenbrook way of life come to the edge of extinction. Those who remain recall those who have gone. Tony, broken by the death of young Hanno, wonders if somewhere there will be a reunion: 'Life crushes so much in us, it destroys so many of our beliefs—a reunion— if it were so . . .' It is left to the hunch-backed teacher Sesemi Weichbrodt to sound the note of affirmation:

'It is so,' she said, with her whole strength; and looked at them with a challenge in her eyes.

She stood there, a victor in the good fight which all her life she had waged against the assaults of Reason: hump-backed, tiny, quivering with the strength of all her convictions, a little prophetess, admonishing and inspired.[17]

Her conviction reflects the artistic intention underlying the work. Mann's detailed involvement and detached scrutiny of the Buddenbrook family gives to them the permanence which art bestows. When we stand back to review the decline of the family, we see the pattern of what he has achieved in the process of time and the accumulation of circumstance. The recurrent leitmotifs of the sea, of houses, of arrival and departure, of birth, marriage and death, fix the fortunes of this particular family in the flow of life itself. All that has been achieved through the long labour of conscious intention to clarify and preserve stands itself as a monument of the artist's will against a sense of decline. In his writing Mann had lived up to the reputation of his ancestors— and, displaying many of their virtues, had added honour to the respect in which they were held.

In three tales, written after *Buddenbrooks*, Mann returns to the theme of the demands of the artist's life—not as autobiography, but as a defence of its intention and end. These tales are apologies for art; and they give to it a value which in a time of decadence and sensationalism it might appear to be losing. Mann places himself in the tradition of those great writers who have schooled and disciplined themselves in their art, until, in spite of themselves, they produce something good. Nothing could be more remote than the notion of art as spontaneous or instinctive; and yet the best of Mann's writing, in spite of its conscious schooling, gives the impression of being both.

The simplest and most graphic account of the artist's life occurs in *A weary hour*. Late at night, cold and gloomy, the writer sits up, considering his unfortunate conception, aware that it is hopelessly wrong. After years of struggle as an intellectual freebooter, he has achieved a position of civic dignity, and with it a sense that he is exhausted and worn out. He is inspired by love and hatred with the knowledge of his rival at work in Weimar. To him, it seems, creation is an effortless and gushing spring; while to the narrator a sentence was shaped, a hard train of thought followed out only by ceaseless discipline and self-control. In the next room his wife sleeps; as he watches he tries to explain to her too: 'I love thee so! By God I swear it. It is only that sometimes I am tired out, struggling at my self-imposed task, and my feelings will not respond.' But he knows that in his present mood he must brood no more. He must take up his pen and work, eliminate, fashion, complete. He does just this: 'And being once finished, lo, it was also good.'[18]

In this brief story, distanced by its historical setting, Mann conveys the physical, intellectual and emotional problems of the artist in pursuing his calling. He celebrates his ability to carry the work through to the end, against the odds which weariness and circumstance place in the way. The finely wrought structure of the writing—its detail without clutter, its exact placing of personality in a particular environment and its awareness of the subtlety and complexity of psychological problems—mirrors what the writer within the story is trying to achieve. The cleverness of the piece depends on its ability to remind us that we are actually watching an act of creation, at the same time as reading of an inability to create; and both achieve their culmination and perfection at the same moment. Mann's self-conscious direction of our attention is thus deliberate and effective. The story succeeds in celebrating a real struggle of the will, and its triumph against the odds. In this sense it is moving; but its manner is more conceptual, and so less deeply involving than either *Tonio Kröger* or *Death in Venice*.

Mann's preoccupation with the nature of the artist's achievement in these two stories contrasts sharply with his depiction of the false artist in *Tristan*. Detrich Spinell's self-indulgence manifests itself in a number of ways: his persistent rereading of his own work, his aestheticism and pedantry, and the alleged 'feeling for style' which makes him seclude himself in the sanatorium. Such feeling is scarcely borne out by the tasteless and ridiculous letter which he writes to Herr Klötterjahn about his wife, nor in his reaction to Klötterjahn's understandable disgust and anger. The story ends with the observation: 'His gait was the hesitating gait of one who would disguise the fact that, inwardly, he is running away.'[19] Spinell does not lack sensitive appreciation of art; but as in the case of Christian in *Buddenbrooks*, this expresses a retreat from life—in contrast to the real artist's direct attack upon it. The heroism of Thomas Buddenbrooks in its initial thrust and self-discipline has much more in common with the struggle of Tonio Kröger and von Aschenbach than they have with those who like to think of themselves as artists, but in fact are not. Even so, *Tonio Kröger* and *Death in Venice* view the artist's struggle from rather different perspectives. *Tonio Kröger* is an exterior work, concerned with the artist's exclusion from the normality and affections for which he yearns, but which cannot be made to coincide with his art; *Death in Venice* with the awakening of passion in an artist who has long denied himself out of a relentless dedication.

Tonio Kröger follows the life of an artist from the first love of childhood to mature middle age when the problems of an established and isolated life, relentlessly dedicated, make him long for the normality of ordinary affections and activities. This love of the commonplace, 'the blond and the blue-eyed, the fair and the living, the happy and the lovely', nourishes his art, because it is not altogether free of contempt. The discipline which had gone into sustaining a novel of the length of *Buddenbrooks* is differently valuable here, in the unhurried compression that makes for depth without extensiveness. The portrait of Tonio Kröger investigates the special nature of the artist's existence—but sees it as composed of experiences, memories, affections which are common rather than special. The peculiar nature of his role derives rather from the price he must pay to give form to his experience. 'He worked, not like a man who works that he may live; but as one who is bent on doing nothing but work; having no regard for himself as a human being, but only as a creator. . . .'[20]

In time this arouses a disgust with the struggle to depict life without having any part in it. Literature seems to him not a calling, but a curse; and the life of the artist a form of imprisonment. To society also there seems something shady about his existence; the good name which his family once bore in his own town as wealthy merchants can no longer be invoked by a man of his calling. But this exclusion from society hurts less than a growing sense of being excluded from the party of life. At a ball he sees his first love dancing with the boy who had once been his closest companion, and knows that if he attempts to speak to them they will not understand him: '. . . they would listen like strangers to anything he was able to say. For their speech was not his speech.'[21] His dedication to art has not only deprived him of love, but imposed upon him icy desolation and solitude. He knows that he stands between two worlds, and is happy in neither.

In *Tonio Kröger*, Mann presents the predicament of the artist as a personal lived experience; and every event contributes to our understanding of Kröger's psychological distress. The irony of the early stories has become here a means of probing the creative process, instead of a means of registering life's lacerations. The artist becomes the detached observer of his experience, calculating its import and meaning, aware of the pain it involves—and nonetheless glad of it, because in the end it proves good and fruitful. He cannot live without feeling; but unlike other people he cannot live by his feelings. He has to hold them away from him so that he can transform them into the substance of his art; and this requires that self-sacrificing dedication which is both Kröger's curse and victory. The story embodies a view of art which justifies its claims to be considered a higher calling, since its demands involve a persistent wrestling with experience, and the achievement through that of work that is good.

And yet at another level the story is an image of the price that must be always paid for excellence in any sphere. Kröger's insistence on the importance to him of the commonplace makes the work fall short in effect of the heights which Mann was to reach in *Death in Venice*, where he was able to take the self-indulgence of Aschenbach's passion for Tadzio, and through the alchemy of creation cause to rise from it a structure so well wrought, sublime, and representative that it symbolises in its brief organic unity the depths and splendours of the European spirit.

Death in Venice brings together in a more complex and subtle manner the two themes to which Mann has persistently returned: the pressure and the threat of the passions operating against reason and habit; and the life of the artist as embodying certain specific challenges which it will require all his experience, concentration and tact to overcome. Unlike *Buddenbrooks*, where the value of art is justified in the exactitude and care and affection lavished upon a particular way of life, in *Death in Venice* its value is taken as given, the underlying assumption beneath Aschenbach's fame. But Aschenbach has grown weary with the daily struggle to impose reason and form on experience; he looks towards some new adventure, to renew the fortitude and inspiration necessary in the daily and lonely struggle. As Mann himself put it, 'the problem I especially had in mind was that of the artist's dignity—I wanted to show something like the tragedy of supreme achievement.'[22] The form which the tragedy takes reasserts Mann's already close involvement, as a writer, with the theme of the significance of disease and death.

Aschenbach has achieved renown through ardent self-discipline and will. He has lived for his work alone, and his books bear witness to the triumph born of his dedication: 'Their creator could hold out for years under the strain of the same piece of work, with an endurance and tenacity of purpose like that which had conquered his native province of Silesia, devoting to actual composition none but his best and freshest hours.'[23] But the relentless self-denial and commitment to lonely, exacting work have taken their toll of Aschenbach—at least within, if not visibly to his public. In need of spiritual refreshment his thoughts turn to the East, and take him, circuitously, to the most fabulous of Western cities, Venice. It is there that the long-suppressed passions, subjugated to the requirements and pursuit of art, are aroused once more by the young Polish boy, Tadzio. But chance alone does not determine that he appears at a moment of weariness and lassitude for the writer. He is the image of Aschenbach's renewal—the youth and beauty which his style is in danger of losing—and which in the life of the artist has recurrently to undergo death in order to return from the dark refreshed. As he sits on the beach watching the boy, Aschenbach finds the springs of his inventiveness and imagination renewed:

> Never had the pride of the word been so sweet to him, never had he known so well that Eros is in the word, as in those perilous and precious hours when he sat at his rude table, within the shade of his awning, his idol full in view and the music of his voice in his ears, and fashioned his little essay after the model Tadzio's beauty had set.[24]

Aschenbach recognises in his love for Tadzio a feeling of shame. When his attempt to leave Venice fails, he is glad on Tadzio's account that this is so. He reflects with remorse on how his ancestors would view his present fervour:

> He thought of them now, involved as he was in this illicit adventure, seized of these exotic excesses of feeling; thought of their stern self-command and decent manliness and gave a melancholy smile. What, indeed, would they have said to his entire life that varied to the point of degeneracy from theirs?[25]

What they would see as degeneracy he knows to be the origin of his art: a disease necessary to the attainment of health. The febrility of Eros is welcome because illicit, a blow against the conventions which deaden or obscure the artist's awareness:

> Passion is like crime: it does not thrive on the established order and the common round; it welcomes every blow dealt the bourgeois structure, every weakening of the social fabric, because therein it feels a sure hope of its own advantage.[26]

So the passion is linked on one side with the Asiatic cholera which

Venice itself tries to conceal, and, on the other, with the art to which
Aschenbach's life has been a persistent act of dedication:

> But detachment . . . and preoccupation with form lead to intoxica-
> tion and desire; they may lead the noblest among us to frightful
> emotional excesses, which his own stern cult of the beautiful would
> make him the first to condemn. So they too lead to the bottomless
> pit. . . .

If Aschenbach did not die at the close, *Death in Venice* might well be
his own next work—obliquely autobiographical, and at the same
time an exploration of the artist's consciousness, a vindication of
his attraction for the abyss in the formal perfection of the achieved
work. Aschenbach has no *nostalgie de la boue*; it is not abasement which
attracts him; on the contrary, it is the image of spiritual beauty:

> His eyes took in the proud bearing of that figure there at the blue
> water's edge; with an outburst of rapture he told himself that what
> he saw was beauty's very essence; form as divine thought, the single
> and pure perfection which resides in the mind, of which an image and
> likeness, rare and holy, was here raised up for adoration. . . .[27]

So too at the end of the story, in the few moments before Aschenbach's
death, Tadzio, on the ocean's edge, stands beckoning and pointing
outward 'into an immensity of richest expectation.'[28] Beauty of form in
the boy matches the formal artistry of the story; and both are images
of that spiritual beauty which arise from the abyss. We cannot attribute
the story to Aschenbach—but it is all that he would have wished it to be.
Like the figure of San Sebastian which he admires, the beauty is born
out of torture, in this case the torture taking the form of the knowledge of his own passion, and the disease which threatens the life
of the loved one.

The stature which Mann ascribes to Aschenbach—a stature
recognised by the world—makes possible the spiritual emphasis of the
tale. In the life of a lesser writer, this incident would have had the
value of mere morbidity; but Aschenbach's largeness acts as a catalyst:
his penetrating analytic power, his ability to interpret experience from
the substance of the narrative, they in effect do the narrator's job for
him. This element of analysis and comment makes *Death in Venice* as
impressive as it is. The strengths and powers which Aschenbach
exhibits in his life as an artist are equally exhibited in the story which tells
of his death.

From the earliest tales Mann was concerned with the disrupting and disintegrating effect of passion; but his depiction of it has since become more 'self-conscious'. Not content with an ironically detached observation of its operation upon the lives of his characters, he now takes it up more subjectively and directly in its relationship to art and the artist's life. This modification is to have much bearing upon the nature of *The Magic Mountain* and *Dr. Faustus* at a later date; it also establishes a link with the theme of the third part of this book: the quest for self. Although Mann in his early works says much implicitly about this, he belongs here as a writer who succeeded in evolving, from a pre-occupation with bizarre and morbid states, an art which celebrates life in its completeness—not, as he said, by writing dithyrambs upon it, but by making us aware through his ampleness and control of victory over those passions which lie at the centre of life, and threaten it with degeneracy. He did not do this, like his contemporary Max Nordau, by attempting to wish them away, or limiting their relevance; but by confronting them in their power and attractiveness. Like Goethe, with whom Mann felt a close spiritual affinity, his finest work is Faustian, involving a triumph over consciousness, in its negative and destructive aspects. He comments aptly upon the nature of his own achievement, and its relevance to the art of celebration when he sums up Aschenbach's work in the following way:

> Forbearance in the face of Fate, beauty constant under torture, are not merely passive. They are a positive achievement, an explicit triumph; and the figure of Sebastian is the most beautiful symbol, if not of art as a whole, yet certainly of the art we speak of here.[29]

Part Three: the quest for self

To live is to war with the troll in caverns of heart and skull.
                                                    Henrik Ibsen

6

HENRIK IBSEN

At a time when the authority of external beliefs and institutions is declining, the individual is inevitably forced back on his own resources, and the defences which he can discover or invent to prevent himself becoming immersed in the void by which he feels himself surrounded. The 'fallings from him, vanishings' do not only alter his relation to the outside world, they alter his relation to himself. In Thomas Mann's case, the particular challenge of being an artist lay in achieving a disciplined and articulated victory over the disorder of existence. But Mann's magisterial tone partly obscures the dangers which have to be avoided if the creative imagination is to remain representative. The randomness within personality can suggest paths which lead in the direction of greater assurance and conviction; equally it can lead to breakdown and disbelief in personality. The artist faces these problems in a particularly acute way, since his art, unsupported by any easily discoverable cultural assumptions, has to find a perspective which is more than personal allegory, and yet not blatantly partisan or provincial. The inherent limitations of self-exploration as a basis for art are exemplified at one extreme by Oscar Wilde, declaring his genius; and at the other by the recurrent insanity of August Strindberg. A brief account of the difficulties which each experienced will provide a standard for evaluating the achievement of those writers who found a way between these extremes; and will also help to create the perspective in which I wish to examine Ibsen's drama.

Wilde lived for sensation; and as each sensation brought him pleasure or pain, joy or sorrow, he savoured it for its particular quality and appraised it for the insight it brought:

The artistic life is simply self-development. Humility in the artist is his frank acceptance of all his experiences, just as love in the artist is simply the sense of beauty that reveals the world its body and soul.[1]

Beauty of form, whether in people, prose style or the passing moment gave to his mind a fervour and power of admiration that few have equalled. Art in anything from cabbages to Chopin aroused in him an intense delight, a desire to praise and enjoy. Like Traherne—but without Traherne's need to interpret the symbol—Wilde rejoiced and delighted in the world of the senses, whether they ranged over all creation, or were restricted to the 'little tent of blue' above Reading Gaol.

But since art meant self-development, the love of beauty was not only to be valued for its own sake. Sensation and the life of the senses gave his life a dynamic: the experience of moments, as they passed, opened up new horizons. The epigram itself was a mode of development: the art of expressing oneself as clearly as possible in order to see as vividly as possible. 'Evolution is the law of life,' he once wrote, and 'there is no evolution except towards individualism.'[2] All the talents of his intellect and his imagination served this end; the individualism of Wilde was used to explore the self—and to recognise finally its limitations.

Towards the beginning of *The Picture of Dorian Gray*, Lord Henry Wotton remarks: 'The aim of life is self-development. To realise one's nature perfectly—that is what each of us is here for.'[3] Gray's possession of wealth gives him the freedom to do so. But what he realises emerges as a monster—callous, murderous, cruel. While Gray's youth and beauty remain unblemished, Basil Hallward's portrait of him registers the degradation of his soul; and when Gray murders Hallward for what he has seen, the portrait records that too. Confronted by the portrait, Gray cannot help recognising the evil within him; and the knowledge of that evil proves unbearable to him. A new life, free from the pleasures and perversions of the old is what he desires. But in stabbing the portrait he kills himself; and the body when found shows a man 'withered, wrinkled and loathsome of visage'. In attempting to realise himself, Gray has succeeded neither in 'curing the soul by means of the senses, or the senses by means of the soul'.[4] He has brought to light the evil within him, and been destroyed by it.

Dorian Gray is a powerful fable, expressing a serious and important view of things. Wilde had sharply experienced the vindictiveness, meanness and violence in human nature; and his exploration of himself went a good deal deeper than the brilliant façade often suggested. Wilde's superabundant intelligence was part of an uncommonly profound mind. *Dorian Gray* amuses, instructs, disturbs, horrifies; and yet it fails—unlike *Death in Venice*—to rank as a great *novella*, because the style is too intent upon itself, never liberating the reader's imagination, and always seeking admiration for its cleverness and profusion. Such admiration is freely granted. *Dorian Gray* ranks among the most original short fictions in the language. And yet a comparison with *Death in Venice* (even in translation) reveals a thinness in the words themselves, because they so obviously solicit praise for the talents of the writer. To enjoy *Dorian Gray* we have to be in the mood for Wilde himself; and this in turn suggests how the problem of personality, even when deeply explored and suggestively represented, can limit and provincialise the experience of the work. That Wilde himself knew this, or came to know it, is well enough borne out by *De Profundis*, published five years after his death in 1900.

No one could fail to be moved by this account of Wilde's suffering at the time of his trial, and later in prison. Mocked and jeered at in public, deprived like other prisoners of ordinary human decencies, judged unfit to see his children, and cut off from almost all intellectual nourishment, Wilde's fall was pitiable and terrible. Wilde knew what caused his fall, and also what lessons it involved for him: 'Tired of being on the heights, I deliberately went to the depths in search for new sensation . . . I ceased to be lord over myself.'[5] The 'perverse' pleasures which came to dominate him left him 'with the possibility of absolute humility, and with the knowledge that nothing in the whole world is meaningless.'[6] Recognition, though, was not enough, since the artistic life meant self-development:

> I am far more of an individual than I ever was. Nothing seems to me of the smallest value except what one gets out of oneself. My nature is seeking a fresh mode of self-realisation. That is all I am concerned with. And the first thing I have got to do is to free myself from any possible bitterness of feeling against the world.[7]

The conventional consolations of religion, reason and morality provided him no help: 'When I think about religion at all, I feel as if I would like to found an order for those who *cannot* believe.'[8] In keeping with this individualism, the only religion he could conceive of was one in which the symbols were of his own making. For the artist, as for men generally, self-realisation means never knowing where one is going, since the 'final mystery is oneself'. But he has also come to the end of his belief in the self, and the sensations by which it is developed:

> I am conscious now that, behind all this beauty, satisfying though it may be, there is some spirit hidden of which the painted forms

and shapes are but modes of manifestation . . . The Mystical in Art,
The Mystical in Life, the Mystical in Nature, this is what I am
looking for . . .[9]

Wilde believed it imperative to find it; but if he did, he did not live
to give expression to it in Art.

Although Wilde finally abandoned his belief in the value of sensations, they served as his most important possession and instrument of
self-understanding. Through them he was able to celebrate the artist
as the creator of beautiful things, and beautiful things as the educators
of the senses. They also made him aware of the Heaven and Hell which
every individual bore within him; and in his art he sought not only to
express this, but to find some means of resolving the tension between
them. Whether his mind turned to politics, history or art, he believed
that 'behind everything that is wonderful stands the individual.' The
idea contained much truth; but as it operated upon his art, it proved a
restrictive force, resulting in too much emphasis on personality as
opposed to humanity, and making the art-work itself self-regarding.

August Strindberg, at the other extreme, always lacked Wilde's
belief in himself. His long and tortured career as a writer and artist
bore witness to his continuous and unsuccessful attempts to understand
and integrate the multiple aspects of his personality. By turns, novelist,
scientist, philologist, alchemist, dramatist, poet, philosopher, painter,
he inquired of everything which might provide him with the certainty
he lacked. 'The greatest thing', he wrote, 'any man can possess (is)
belief in himself';[10] even in his last play, *The Great Highway* (1909), he
admitted how this conviction had eluded him. He had not 'been the
one he had longed to be'.[11] But failure to reach the goal never caused
Strindberg to flag in the strenuousness and inventiveness of his quest.
Sceptical by temperament to the point of self-destruction, he still sought
relentlessly in himself for an answer to the problem posed by a human
world dominated by the struggle for existence—and which he himself
experienced acutely in his struggle to realise himself against the torments
of paranoia and manic depression.

Strindberg's major works as a dramatist—his historical plays excepted
—form two distinctive groups: those plays created directly out of his
fundamental insecurity; and those which seek an answer to the problem
of self-doubt in a comprehensive philosophy. Interesting as the second
group are, they amount to a less considerable artistic achievement than
the first, and provide further evidence of how severe a task confronted

the artist when he tried to resolve, as Wilde finally did, the problem of a limited personal experience. And yet, as in Wilde's case, the immersion in personality also proved a restrictive influence—though for very different reasons.

Strindberg's tormented first marriage to the actress Siri von Essen inspired the substance of his first two important plays: *The Father* and *Miss Julie*. Each is concerned with the conflict which sexual life involves, more especially as it plays upon the individual's fears about his own identity. The conflict between the sexes is conceived as deadly: the weaker personality goes to the wall, whether by loss of reason or suicide. The savageness of the battle is depicted as springing from self-doubt, and the problem of knowing who one is, when one's life becomes deeply involved with that of another human being. The madness of the father in the first play is precipitated by his wife's working upon his doubt as to the true paternity of their child. His deepest anguish springs from the realisation that absolute certainty can never be achieved: a recognition which relates not only to his personal predicament but, in a more general sense, to the human condition. As his wife plays upon his misgivings, he slips inevitably towards madness; the self lacks the strength to resist the forces which prey upon its stability. The play's effectiveness springs from two main sources: the single-minded fierceness with which Strindberg conceives of marital relationships, and the deadly speed with which the action is worked out. But the savage light of the play does not obscure the intensity achieved by narrowness; and the central, but nonetheless limited, view of relationships on which it depends for its speed and *vraisemblance*.

In spite of its wider scope and range of reference, *Miss Julie* suffers from a similar limitation. The aristocratic Miss Julie's desire for the valet Jean is explained by a variety of means: the festive atmosphere of midsummer night, her menstrual cycle, the intoxicating effect of music, and her father's absence. The play's tension is generated by all that results from the gratification of their mutual desire, since it enables Jean to make use (or attempt to make use) of Julie's social position for his own advancement. Julie comes to realise the impossibility of her position: she has no money to leave her father's house; without money Jean has no hope of a future elsewhere; but they cannot remain in her father's household together. When he suggests, by decapitating her pet bird, that death alone provides a release, he turns her thoughts in a direction already half-perceived. Aided by his hypnotic power over her, he needs only to supply a razor for her to be willing to solve their problem by suicide.

The play is once again extremely taut in its construction. The interaction of class-struggle and sexual conflict is contrived with deftness. Julie, in her dream of falling off the top of a pillar, betrays the anxieties of her own emotional life, while expressing precisely the changed nature of her relationship to Jean. The introduction of the class-struggle also deepens the perspective in which the sexual relationships are seen. At the end Jean has got rid of a potential embarrassment in an extraordinarily unpleasant manner; but his prospects have not been improved. Julie's fall from a position of apparent strength and social superiority to suicidal paralysis reflects Strindberg's conviction of the abysses which underlie a sense of identity. The individual has nothing firm to hold on to. Even Jean himself, who appears to dominate, and to win, is lost when it comes to decisions about how he should live, and what he should do. But as with *The Father*, the piece impresses by the savageness of its vision, rather than by its completeness or truth. Strindberg has taken what he does know (which is negative and destructive) and moulded it into a piece of which the effect is tormenting. But the achievement is won by a ruthless excision of all those areas of experience that have no place in a vision as savage as this; and this ruthlessness diminishes the importance of the achievement.

Strindberg's more positive works, though they have gained in scope, lack any real conviction because, as he admitted, no one point of view was capable of satisfying his many-sided personality. As the central character in *The Road to Damascus* admits, 'the whole of life consists of nothing but contradictions';[12] and he is described as 'a wanderer on the quicksands of life,'[13] prepared to follow anyone who can teach him something. He suffers from an everchanging sense of identity, and a loss of a sense of location. Episodic, fragmentary, the action of the play stumbles towards self-understanding, time and again conveying the strain upon the mind which tries to create order out of the disorder of experience. Strindberg's quest for self revealed to him the self's instability and insufficiency; but he could not discover a metaphysic strong enough—at least in his art—to alleviate that knowledge. At times, as in *Easter* and *A Dream Play*, he seems to come close to it; but in each case his vision falls short of real commitment. The redemptive aspects of Christianity, like the growing castle which bursts into flower, suggesting the possibility of a new and more wholesome awareness, sing to him for a while, but do not offer satisfaction. Like Hölderlin's *Hyperion*, Strindberg was driven mad by his failure to find any absolute faith.

In one of his last plays, *The Ghost Sonata* (1907), the Colonel lives with his wife, The Mummy, giving tea-parties for those who have nothing to say to each other, and silent themselves because neither believes what the other one says. The house is dead, except in the hyacinth room where the young girl entertains the student. Even there, the curse of the house eventually falls: young life blighted by the deadness which surrounds it, and overshadowed by the gigantic cook who saps the nourishment out of the food before it is served. Christian music, a Buddha, Böcklin's painting of 'The Isle of the Dead' testify to the existence of a spiritual life, or at least to its possibility—but only as fragments within a fragmented consciousness, close to Strindberg's own. Starting from profound scepticism about the nature of his own identity, Strindberg strove to overcome his uncertainty, and failed. His quest to discover himself estranged him from others, making him in their eyes often a lunatic, while they became in his a threat to his existence, or spectres in a dead parade.

Wilde and Strindberg exemplify two extreme manifestations of the problems which immersion in the self created for the artist. Deprived of external assurances, he became involved not only in the self's chameleon guises, but also in its limitations as an interpreter of truth. However wide-ranging or probing, its revelations could appear to him incomplete, while he was compelled, at the same time, to reject all conventional methods of resolving that incompleteness. In the art of Ibsen, Chekov and E. M. Forster, the theme of self-realisation plays an important part—though the emphasis upon it, and its manifestation, differ as much as might be expected among men of such varied nationality and temperament. All three succeeded, however, in distancing the theme through their art, and avoiding, in varying degrees, the impasse to which Wilde and Strindberg had come.

Ibsen's reputation is founded upon his ability to put ourselves in our own situations on the stage. But his achievement as an observer and portrayer of human nature differs from that of Shakespeare, Dickens or the Tolstoy of *War and Peace* in that the boundaries of his art are far more rigid: his characters, for all their variety and individuality, appear in a drama whose underlying assumptions remain constant from

D

his first play, *Catiline*, written in 1849, when he was twenty-one, to
When We Dead Awaken, which belongs to the final year of the nineteenth century. Ibsen's art deepens, matures, and changes, but always
around a nucleus of attitudes which express his view of the individual
in relation to himself, and society. The individual, in order to live,
'must war with the troll in caverns of heart and skull'; he must also
rebel against the forms of authority, and institutions which stand in the
way of self-realisation ('the strongest man in the world is he who stands
most alone.'[14]) Without metaphysical beliefs, the individual has to
endure a solitary struggle not only against tangible obstructions—
like the conventional social attitudes to religion and marriage—but
against inhibitions of whose nature he may be unaware. Ibsen perceived
that society needed to be transformed; but for him the only possible
way of salvation lay in an inner revolution, by means of which the
individual might realise his highest potential.

George Bernard Shaw, his most notable apologist and populariser,
saw in his works a model of what the theatre should be: 'a temple of
the ascent of man'. But Shaw's belief in evolutionary progress through
socialism was far from Ibsen's own convictions. 'It seems to me,' he
once remarked, 'that the whole history of the world is one colossal
shipwreck, and that the only thing to do is to save oneself from it.' This
extreme individualism went with his rejection of political movements:

> I shall never agree to identify Freedom with political freedom. What
> you call Freedom, I call freedoms, and what I call the battle for
> Freedom is nothing but the continuous pursuit of the idea of
> Freedom.[15]

This quest also embodied the means by which the individual discovered who he was; and Ibsen portrayed this in a drama which
remained as poetic as his philosophy. Paradoxically, though regarded
as the foremost practitioner of naturalism, Ibsen never ceased to be a
poet of the quality which his verse-dramas, *Brand* and *Peer Gynt* had
revealed—works, which, though not intended for the stage, established
his reputation. Both in his powers of association, and in the intensity of
his exploration of the inner life, he remained close to the pure verbal
artist; but he possessed in addition the skill to adapt these gifts to the
particular needs of the theatre. From *Brand* onwards, Ibsen's dramatic
skills expressed themselves through a vivid sense of Norwegian life, a
mastery of varied characterisation, and a restless intellectual questioning
of the nature of existence. But the three are not finally separable, since

Ibsen does not, like Shaw, impose his ideas on his characters, nor make them propagandists for his own views. Rather he conceives life as involving conflicts between individuals, the nature of which illuminates the quality of their inner lives. In *Brand*, the questions at issue are much more clearly defined than they were later to become, while the play is also more loosely structured. As Ibsen's vision of the obscurities and mists in human personality deepened, so the form of his plays grew denser, until they achieved the inevitability of tragedy.

Ibsen's unsuccessful dramatic apprenticeship, which lasted until his mid-thirties, was spent in an environment where by European standards the theatrical possibilities were crude. In Bergen and Christiania he worked in theatres whose technical equipment was as old-fashioned as the tastes of the audience were unsophisticated. Frustrating as this was, it allowed Ibsen's talents to develop without the deadening influence of fashion, and enabled him to observe Norwegian life while still largely unaffected by the complex changes at work in industrialised Europe. When, in addition, he went into exile in Italy, he freed himself from involvement in contemporary events, and was able to reflect upon the local scene with detachment. All these factors contributed to the objectivity and lucidity of vision in his plays; but they also enabled him to pursue the quest for self in isolation. His achievement lay in his ability to translate that experience back into the lives of those he had left behind in Norway.

Brand expresses the ambiguity of that experience more directly than any of his later works. Its central character was, as he said, 'himself in his own best moments'. But *Brand* does not attract an undivided sympathy. His estimate of the human situation as one in which a man must live by his own standards absolutely, if he is to survive, excludes him from social affections, and builds an 'Ice-church' in his heart.

Ibsen uses an episodic structure in the play to portray the vicissitudes and tests through which Brand must pass, in order to harden his will in the service of becoming what he is. His mother dies unconsoled by the sacraments he will not administer unless she gives up her worldly wealth; his child dies because he will not forsake his 'flock', and take the boy to a healthier climate; his wife dies, broken in spirit, by his relentless will. Ibsen's dramatic skill manifests itself in the conflict he establishes between Brand's lonely struggle with himself, and the conventional attitudes of those he encounters: the Doctor, the Mayor, the Painter and the unnamed villagers. They expose the defects of his absolutism, as he reveals the unacceptability of their compromise. The play does not permit a simple response to Brand, or the villagers. Brand can never see that in a human world all individual values, however absolutely held, remain relative, while they are blind to the impoverishment of their inner lives through compromise.

But the outlook of the play is not one of despair. As a man, Brand offends the deepest notions of humanity: his single-mindedness seems more the mark of a limited personality than of a real visionary. But as a visionary he compels assent to the view that life should free itself of petty and trivial considerations; his journey into the mountains reveals an impressive integrity, even if the methods he uses and the ends to which he comes display all the folly of human pride. By means of its extremely loose structure, the play succeeds in presenting the price which must be paid for any change in the attitudes by which men live, and the necessity for such a change if the conditions of existence are to be improved. Only at the very end does Ibsen's artistry fail in clarity. The voice which calls from the destructive avalanche 'He is the God of love'[16] does not answer the problems which Brand has posed, except by a traditional Christian view of suffering that is discordant with the anarchic tone of the previous action.

Peer Gynt complements the achievement of *Brand*. *Brand* exposes the limitations of the self; *Peer Gynt* explores its dreams, and illusions. Peer is driven by a desire to discover the 'Gyntian self', whatever the cost to others. His lifelong quest compels him to perceive the error of assuming the self has a centre. When, near his journey's end, Peer peels an onion, he discovers to his horror that it has no heart; and the point strikes home:

> So a soul can go back, so wretchedly poor
> Into the grey mists of nothingness.
> Beautiful earth, do not be angry
> That I have trod you and left no mark
> Beautiful sun, you have squandered your light,
> Your glorious light on an empty house.
> There was no one within to be heartened and cheered,
> The owner had gone . . .[17]

This is a moment of real bleakness. But Ibsen's inventiveness throughout the play—his humour, his sustained poetic power and his awareness of everyday life—has created a dramatic action more exuberant than pessimistic. Peer experiences life as a buoyant adventure, until old age and the fear of death fall upon him. Selfish, vain, rakish, cowardly, he remains likeable for his resourcefulness, and his ability, however super-ficial, to savour and enjoy. In the light of these qualities, the final revelation of the emptiness of his self-regard becomes the more serious.

The play also conceives of an answer to that emptiness in the love of Solveig, who has waited for his return in the mountains: a love from which he has run because in his pride and vanity he sees himself as un-worthy of it. At a representational level, Solveig has too many of the qualities of a mother for easy acceptance in a Freudian age; but taken more symbolically, she represents the possibility of a solution to the self's inadequacy and isolation. Her faith, hope and love stand against the emptiness Peer has discovered in himself: the symbol of his largest and least conscious victory.

Both *Brand* and *Peer Gynt* use the inner life of the individual as the source of dramatic action; the plays that followed, though they centred on the conflict between individuals, and the nature of their relation-ships, continued to see that conflict in the light of the individual's need to discover himself.

Pillars of Society was finished in 1877. In its social aspect the play dealt with the hollow morality upon which the apparent respectability of the leading citizens in a small Norwegian town was based. Ibsen skilfully combines the mounting tension of the scandal over the acquisition of land for the railway, bought up by Karsten Bernick while he pretends to oppose the scheme, with the gradual revelation of the corruption on which his career has been built. Financial necessity has determined even Bernick's marriage, at the expense of the woman to whom he was already engaged, and later of his wife's happiness. When, in the final act, the citizens come to honour their most respected member, he is compelled to dampen their rejoicing by confessing his corruption and guilt. He is inspired by the hope that though he, like the rotten society to which he belongs may be destroyed, a generation may grow up not cursed by the same hypocrisies and greed. But he is also inwardly driven towards his confession by the woman who loved him in his youth, and knows the extent of the lies on which his success has been built. In her desire to see the hero of her youth stand 'free and true', Lona Hessel compels Bernick to face his real self, and in doing so to save his marriage as well as his moral identity. Without truth to self

Ibsen conceives living relationships with others as ceasing to be possible; but equally 'salvation' can only come from within.

Ibsen's concern with inner values transforms his play from a drama of situation in the manner of Wilde's *An Ideal Husband* into a more complex and involving statement about the necessity for inner integrity. Ibsen's poetic power of association, and of thinking in concrete images, is responsible here for much of the play's effectiveness. He uses his numerous dramatic characters to reveal the community's moral hollowness from various but interlocking perspectives. Bernick's own rottenness is mirrored in his willingness to let *The Indian Girl* sail while knowing her to be unseaworthy. The image of the ship inadequately repaired, and unable to stand up to an ocean storm, figuratively suggests the effect on Bernick of his lifetime's deceits. Its symbolic force is further heightened when Bernick's son is thought to have stowed away in the company of the man whose good name Bernick has sullied to save his own reputation.

Ibsen has learnt to fuse the poetic and the dramatic, so as to create a play of external tensions, while never allowing his audience to forget their relevance to the moral world within. Bernick's confession of his guilt permits too the poetic justice of his son's return, and the countermanding of the order for *The Indian Girl* to sail. In addition to the verbal artistry which associates the different levels of the action, Ibsen also uses the stage to amplify his meaning. The opening of the curtains across Bernick's windows in Act Four to let in the light of the procession seems initially an irony, since Bernick's real life has never been open to public view; the image the crowd have come to honour does not exist. But it also symbolises the much more important light which is beginning to dawn within him. *The Pillars of Society* may appear at first sight to be concerned with public life and values; but its action springs from the private world, where Ibsen saw the central victories as being won or lost.

A Doll's House (1879) also celebrates, in a more domestic manner, Nora's release from the lies and deceits which have stifled her life. Seized upon by the feminist movement, *A Doll's House* was in fact no more propagandist than *Pillars of Society*. Nora is compelled to leave her husband and children in order to discover who she really is. Such knowledge of herself would provide the only basis for marriage to Torvald, or anyone else. Ibsen contrasts the sudden awareness of inner necessity in Nora with her husband's unchanging complacency,

which expresses itself in his prejudices about the proper way for a wife
to behave, and what he as a husband can expect from her. The shock of
her going is a blow to his conventions, but not to his view of himself.
Torvald, like the villagers in *Brand*, has lost the desire to change; and
the 'miracle of miracles' which would make a real marriage between
him and Nora possible remains a remote chance because this is so. His
calling her his 'little song-bird' expresses all too accurately the role he
expects her to play, while her secretive eating of the macaroons,
against his orders, hints at the life she has to conceal because it conflicts
with Torvald's view of how she ought to be.

From simple verbal and visual devices of this kind, Ibsen initiates a
drama which will explore the gulf between Torvald and his wife. The
ominous shadow of the I.O.U., and later, of the letter in which
Krogstad will reveal his knowledge of Nora's forgery, become the
theatrically effective instruments for conveying the degree to which
Torvald's attitudes have driven his wife to subterfuge; and her
fevered dancing of the tarantella expresses for her part the increasingly
intolerable burden of the situation. She is literally dancing to save her
life with Torvald by preventing him from reading the letter; but her
dancing also expresses metaphorically the desire for release from the
strain. At the time she thinks this will come by suicide; in fact it occurs
through her leaving him—again a theatrical reversal of considerable
effectiveness.

Without this degree of verbal and dramatic skill in investing everyday objects and activities with the power to mirror inner realities,
Ibsen could only have written a discussion play on the subject of the
liberation of women. Intellectually stimulating as this might have been,
it could not have involved the audience in Nora's movement towards
understanding her real needs, nor would it have conveyed that elation
at release from pressure which flows from her confrontation with
Torvald. By his use of poetic association, as for instance in the dance,
Ibsen makes us *feel* the necessity for Nora's departure. Her slamming of
the front door was heard all over Europe, not only because of its
defiance of convention, but because Ibsen had succeeded by these means
in making it seem an act of triumphant rightness—at least, for her. In
his later works Ibsen was to find this celebration of the potentially fulfilled and realised self harder to achieve, because of his growing awareness that the self could not always discover its real nature as clearly as
Bernick and Nora suggested.

The Wild Duck marks the beginning of this new period of Ibsen's dramatic development. The symbol of the title radiates out through the play, integrating the action and identifying a common human characteristic, which expresses itself in diverse ways. It refers to the behaviour of the wild duck which, when wounded, dives to the bottom of the lake, holds on to the seaweed, and never comes up to the surface again. The behaviour of the wild duck represents the mirror-image of that absolute will to express oneself portrayed in *Brand*; and the play exemplifies the tragic effects of adopting this mode of behaviour. But Ibsen has now begun to deal in deeper psychological truths than in his portrait of the compromised villagers. The wrong kind of compromise has ceased to be a moral defect, and become the sign of a psychological disability.

Blindness is the play's controlling image. Hedvig's impaired sight is inherited from her real father, but all the major characters suffer from it in some form. Blindness for them consists in not knowing that they are wounded, and in behaving like the wild duck without consciousness of doing so. Such a defect makes it impossible to discover one's real self, or even to desire the freedom to do so. Gregers Werle pursues the claims of the ideal, failing to see either his own moral inadequacy for reforming others, or the danger of confronting them with truths they will not be able to bear. Hjalmar Ekdal, his victim, already mimics the wild duck in his belief that the family's fortunes will be saved by his invention; Gregers' revelation that he is not the father of his own child causes him to believe that he can no longer love her: an even severer manifestation of the same disease. And it precipitates the tragedy of Hedvig supposing that her father's love can be restored by sacrificing the wild duck, and finally becoming herself the offering to his anger. In this play Ibsen has reversed the development of the dramatic action in *A Doll's House*. There, he dramatised a solution to the problems of family relationships by splitting them apart; here he conceives their subtly interlocked structure as causing a catastrophe—the more terrible since the sacrificed life is that of a child.

The direction which Ibsen's drama had taken in *The Wild Duck* was formative for the later plays. The increasing density of the writing, arising out of the creation of characters who often do not, or cannot, express what they are feeling, reflected his preoccupation with the emotional complexities of individual life. In *Rosmersholm*, in particular, he achieved a drama which, while not losing anything in particularity of characterisation, was sounding depths in personality which lay well beneath the articulate. Freud's analysis of the childhood inhibition which causes Rebecca West to reject Rosmer's proposal of marriage with such violence carries conviction; but it also strays beyond what can be verified by reference to the play. And for all its interest it does finally seem superfluous. In *Rosmersholm*, the suicide of Rebecca and Rosmer results from the labyrinth of emotions which the characters themselves do not fully understand; their strength is intuitively detected by the audience, but their origin never precisely identified. Rebecca feels that Rosmer's sexless love has ennobled her, but destroyed her happiness; Rosmer that they can only become man and wife when the guilt of Beata's death has been expiated. By killing herself to make way for their love, Beata has also ensured that it cannot be fulfilled. To Mrs. Helseth their joint suicide appears as the wages of sin; but to them it presages the start of their marriage. As a ritual act it may be taken as the means of purifying those emotions which have prevented their union; as a physical fact it represents the tragic culmination of their inability to resolve the nature of their involvement in any other way. What they choose to call ennobling means a failure to confront and resolve their individual responsibilities and their relationship to each other.

Here again, Ibsen works through images which suggest the nature of his characters' inner world. The mill-race reminds Rebecca and Rosmer of their guilt; but it is also suggestive of the dangerous and inhibited flow of their sexual lives. The white horse, which appears as a warning of death, belongs to that spectral level of existence where their be-haviour is determined; and in its whiteness it presages the release and the purification from guilt they will find in death. In setting too, the curtained and oppressive house where nobody laughs is of a piece with Rebecca's and Rosmer's withdrawal from life, and is contrasted with the sunlit park beyond. Much of Ibsen's power derives from the ability to write simultaneously about the actual world, and about the world within, however deeply submerged. Truth to self is essential in both; and in this play, unlike *Pillars of Society*, and *A Doll's House*, it proves unattainable.

When Thomas Mann observed in relation to *Buddenbrooks* that 'every good book that is written against life is actually tempting its readers on behalf of life',[18] he was also commenting shrewdly on Ibsen. His world is not tragic by necessity, but only by default. Skill and wisdom are capable of preventing disaster, just as the wrong kind

of pressure—such as that exerted by Judge Brack on Hedda Gabler—
is capable of precipitating it. One of his most persuasively poetic works,
The Lady from the Sea (1888) shows his continuing ability to write with
a positive emphasis. Ellida Wangel suffers from a severe psychological
illness which prevents her from living with her husband; in the past she
has met a mysterious sailor who has claimed her as his bride; and as a
symbol of their union has thrown the ring with which he has married
her into the sea. Even though she has attempted to end the symbolic
union, he has ignored her pleas, and confirmed that one day he will
return to claim his bride. Set in a garden on the edge of a fjord to which
the ships come and go, the play is pervaded by Ibsen's awareness of the
Norwegian landscape, and the lives of its people: seafarers who live
beside fjords, isolated in their communities and families, and susceptible
to dreams. Ellida finds the fjord a suffocating place: her thoughts flow
back to the sea in which the sailor is supposed drowned. The power
that he continues to exert over her is wrought from a fabric of
associations. When they were together, they talked mainly of the sea;
even the pearl in his tie-pin seemed like a dead fish's eye; and now in
his absence her haunting longing for the sea marks his power over her
soul.

As always in Ibsen, the inner landscape of Ellida's emotional life is
not given to us whole, but grows like a melodic theme from the
relationships and friendships of which family life is composed. At the
same time, the play moves gracefully and relentlessly towards its
climax: the return of the sailor in Act Three to claim his bride. With deft
psychological veracity, Ibsen portrays Ellida as not even recognising him
when he first turns up; but as succumbing to his demand that she must
make her choice of her own free will, for or against him, irrevocably on
the following day; and it is this freedom to choose for herself that Ellida
asks of her husband. The choice in her inmost soul cannot be determined
by anyone outside her. As in Eliot's world, freedom is responsibility;
and that can only be exercised without bondage to others. Once given
the freedom to choose for herself, Ellida finds that the power of the
unknown no longer terrifies or fascinates her. The sailor can be rejected
for the ordinary man he is.

Ibsen succeeds in making out of an implausible situation a work
which communicates through its poetry the lure of Ellida's fantasies,
and the force of the strange impulses working upon her to threaten her
sanity. But the environment in which the haunting is played out re-

mains that of normal relationships. Strindberg rivalled Ibsen in dramatising the torments of the inner life, but could never place them in the context of relationships observed from the outside. For Ibsen, the exercise of responsibility from within, through freedom, was essential if the individual was to survive; and the outcome of that struggle affected the success or failure, the tragedy or happiness of relationships with others. Had Ibsen remained a poet only, he would have pursued this quest for the self in the mythology that best suited his personal identity; instead he dramatised that quest, and the consequences of failing to undertake it, in the lives of men and women, families and communities. Not all Ibsen's characters achieve victory in the struggle as Bernick and Ellida do: the majority go under. But his art does celebrate at least the possibility of victory; and at some level in human personality the intention to achieve it.

Just as Aschenbach becomes weary in the ceaseless discipline of his art, Ibsen registers in his later plays a sorrow that stems more particularly from the predicament of the artist in striving to present his truth. Being innovatory and original as it is, the quest for self isolates him from others, and brings him in the end to an impasse not unlike that of Wilde. The objectification of the struggle in a form as social as Ibsen's drama conceals, but does not cure, the loneliness and the cost of bringing the vision to light; and the figure of the artist himself—except in the final play, thinly disguised—emerges with an increasing melancholy.

To free people from their illusions (which Shaw saw as the major objective of Ibsen's drama) is represented in *The Wild Duck* as a dangerous and misplaced objective. As Dr. Relling points out, it may be better to give people hopes, however false, which enable them to live than truths which destroy them. Gregers Werle in his pursuit of the ideal is conceived as more of a villain than a hero: his wrong-headedness derives as much from his misjudgement of those he is trying to save as from his inadequacies as a moral reformer. In him, Ibsen suggests the predicament of an artist who sees through the false ideals with which society protects itself; but also recognises the disputable wisdom of trying to strip the masks from others.

From *The Wild Duck* on, the figure of the artist recurs in various guises, but always as a disruptive and disquieting force. In *Hedda Gabler*, Eilert Lövborg, the inspired writer, is isolated by his talent (and its manifestation in his wild personality) from society and normal human relationships. His death in a brothel, where he shoots himself through the genitals, may be taken metaphorically as an image of the wounds the artist inflicts on himself. Solness, the Master Builder, thinly disguises the artist whose creative endeavours have led indirectly to an increasing estrangement between him and his wife; and his desire to attempt the impossible in recapturing the power and virility of his youth. In *Little Eyolf*, too, the central character of Almers is portrayed as writing his great work, 'The Responsibility of Man'—a labour which, like his sterile marriage, gives him no satisfaction. His decision to give up the book for the sake of educating his son, and his wife's decision to take in orphaned children after Eyolf is drowned, indicate their acceptance of a real human responsibility, in contrast to the self-absorption of the past. Ibsen's commitment as man and writer to the inner life (and survival) of the individual remains as deep-rooted as ever. He recognises now, though, the cost of that survival—not in the rather crude terms of *Brand*, but in a form which points to the destructive effect of the artist's single-minded concern with his art—not only on himself, but on those closest to him.

And this is the theme of his final play, *When We Dead Awaken*. Here, the artist emerges in his mantle of power as creator, but also as the slayer of the woman he loves, and of his own life, in the service of art. His masterpiece, 'The Day of Resurrection', is their child: a child that he himself has disfigured out of horror at the admiration which the work attracts from those who do not understand it. One part of the dramatic action is concerned with the renewed relationship between the sculptor Rubek and Irene (accompanied by a nun who symbolises the death they have both undergone as the result of his dedication); the other with Maja, the woman with whom he is presently living. His promise to show her 'all the glories of the world' has not been fulfilled; and after her meeting with the hunter Urfleym she sets out to discover with him the freedom and life which exists in the mountains.

Rubek's one hope of resurrection lies with Irene, capable of opening once more the casket to his heart. But she still hates the artist in him who wants to create more than to love, and who once turned their love into stone. Irene believes that their life cannot be resurrected because they have never lived; and yet she too is in search of life, conceived in terms of freedom and awakening.

The last act of the play takes place on a 'wild, broken mountain-top'. Urfleym and Maja are going back to the valley where in the celebration of the life of the senses they belong. Irene and Rubek are to continue their journey together into the mountains. Irene carries the knife with which she will kill anyone who comes up to fetch her, but also the knife with which she would have killed Rubek the day before, if they were not, in her view, both already dead.

Here now in the mountains, they appear transfigured by a new love; below them Maja, whose name suggests illusion, sings 'I am free! I am free!'[19] While she goes down to meet life, Rubek and Irene go up to meet the avalanche which will destroy them. Whatever new realm of being they might have entered, death stands in the way. But the play is nonetheless a step in the direction of a new kind of vision. Neither the claims of the artist, nor the fulfilment of individual needs in the process of self-realisation, are capable of cutting the Gordian knot which binds desirable ends to their destructive means. Man's present state of striving is like a sleep from which he needs to awaken to a higher state of consciousness. Those who come closest to this are those who have realised their own inner lives to the highest degree, though the cost may be high both to others and themselves, and the goal far from reached when Death intervenes.

Ibsen's art from the first play to the last is concerned with the individual's journey towards liberation from the constraints of social conventions, and his own inhibitions. It expresses a deep sympathy with those who strive against the odds to reach the heights. Ibsen saw this as involving the loss of ordinary comforts and consolations, as well as the ruthless stripping of masks and defences. As he grew older, he also saw the intractability of much in the struggle, because it involved getting rid not only of what one could see, but what remained submerged and intangible. In his later works the inhibitions of the unconscious mind conflict tragically with more conscious needs, desires and aspirations. The resolution of this conflict requires the higher consciousness to which the final play is pointing. But the first part of this process still remains the individual's will to become himself—to turn towards the sun and mountains wherever he finds them. The potentiality within the individual for doing this remains Ibsen's most positive affirmation in the struggle for existence. The ore that could be mined within the caverns of heart and skull contained the treasure that he celebrated.

ANTON CHEKOV

What beautiful trees—and how beautiful, when you think of it, life ought to be with trees like these!

Three Sisters, Act Four

Tolstoy once complained to Chekov in conversation: 'You know I cannot abide Shakespeare, but your plays are even worse.'[1] Chekov's plays lacked, in his opinion, a point of view. Chekov, who felt an unequalled love and affection for Tolstoy, admitted the truth in what he was saying; but could not do anything about it.

I have often been blamed, even by Tolstoy, for writing about trifles, for not having any positive heroes . . . but where am I to get them! Our life is provincial, the cities unpaved, the villages poor, the masses abused. In our youth we all chirp rapturously like sparrows on a dung-heap, but when we are forty, we are already old and begin to think of death. Fine heroes we are![2]

In Chekov's view, the life of the individual was all too often unfulfilled and impoverished, spiritually as well as materially. If he had probed more deeply, he might have reached a view of character not unlike Ibsen's in his later works. But Chekov depicted that frustration as the result of forces at work in life and time, without involving himself in its particular emotional or psychological causes. Again, he placed more emphasis on the Russian temperament as an explanation of the tendency to philosophise and delay action, than, for example, upon the influence exerted by heredity which preoccupied Ibsen throughout his life. Chekov's characters too can perceive their defects; and knowing they will not change, they look to future generations to avoid their errors. 'Humanity is perpetually advancing, always seeking to perfect its own powers,'[3] says Trofimov in *The Cherry Orchard*. 'One day all the things that are beyond our grasp at present are going to fall within our reach, only to achieve this we've got to work. . . .'[4] Hope for the future only partly conceals the 'lacrymae rerum'. Although the individual may not be rewarded, he must continue to work, search and hope. Chekov's recognition—not without irony—that this was how many people lived aroused his love and admiration for human beings in their hard and often thankless pilgrimage; this in turn gave to his works a more compassionate tone than was present in Ibsen's.

Unlike Tolstoy, Chekov had none of the advantages of social position to protect him in his youth from coming to know how hard life was for the majority of men. In the small town of Taganrog, on the sea of Azov, where his father kept a general store, Chekov was schooled by the daily struggle for existence. His father worked him long hours in the shop, and bullied the family at home. His incompetence in business, and his religious zeal, inspired mainly by his love of church music, brought neither material comfort nor spiritual joy to his family's life. Compulsory attendance at church made Sundays and holy days dreadful occasions for his children. Anton Chekov was later to say: 'I was brought up in religion, and received a religious education . . . And what is the result? I remember my childhood as a pretty gloomy affair, and I'm not a bit religious now.'[5] In his art, as in his life, Chekov derived no consolation from traditional belief; what he asserted as positive good had to be won against the hard and dull facts of life, as he knew it. The slave, he said, had to be squeezed out of him drop by drop. The characters he created reflected his experience of how much depended on the inner resources of the individual.

After the death of his father, when he was nineteen, Chekov assumed responsibility for his family's finances. While training to become a doctor, he started to write the stories that were later to make him famous. Throughout his life, he continued to believe in the benefits which people would derive from scientific progress and education. Although he came to see himself first as a writer, he continued to practise medicine in times of epidemic, or in cases of want. He was active in setting up local libraries and creating improved facilities in schools. By travelling to the convict settlement on Shakhalin, off the coast of Japan, he sought to bring about an improvement in the conditions he found there. All these activities extended what he wanted to achieve in his writing:

> I only wished to tell people honestly, 'Look at yourselves, see how badly and boringly you live!' The principal thing is that people should understand this, and where they do, they will surely create for themselves another and better life.[6]

Nothing that Chekov experienced—not even the filth, disease and drunkenness of the peasants—tempted him to feel that things could not be improved, but only to question how the same waste might be avoided in the future. The answer which he reflected in his art was a personal one, and depended upon individual endeavour: the will to endure so that in the future life might be better.

Chekov once described Tolstoy's faith as the one closest to his heart, and the one most suited to him. But he could not imagine the idea of non-resistance to evil as being the solution to life as he knew it. In *Ward Number Six*, one of his finest and most sombre stories, Chekov implicitly portrayed the need for active resistance, not only because of the magnitude of social ills; but because if the individual did not resist, he too would be destroyed.

The young doctor, Ragin, posted to a hospital in a rural area, soon concludes it to be an immoral institution, detrimental to the inmates' health. 'In his opinion the best thing to do was to discharge the patients and close the hospital down.'[7] However, he lacks the will-power to fight the inertia and prejudice of the Rural District Council. And anyway, 'clearing away all the physical and moral uncleanliness from one place would merely transfer it to another.'[8] In spite of the conditions, Ragin works hard to begin with, doing the best he can in hopeless circumstances. But in time he becomes bored by the monotony and palpable futility of his work. He begins to let things slide, and ceases to attend hospital every day. In the evenings he consoles himself with books, and the conversation of the postmaster. But he also forms a friendship of sorts with Gromov, a patient in Ward Number Six, where the mentally ill are confined. Gromov likes to argue about metaphysical and philosophic problems; and Ragin argues with him. His prolonged visits to the ward attracts the attention of his envious junior, Khobotov, who secures Ragin's dismissal and eventual confinement in the ward, where he dies.

Through this tale Chekov exposes the ignorance and brutality which characterise life in a provincial Russian town. But he also depicts how Ragin's degradation is brought about by his loss of heart when he fails to resist the evil he clearly sees. In failing to take action he loses both his commitment to his professional life, and in the end his sense of identity; he becomes unable to tolerate either himself or others:

> In former days Dr. Ragin used to spend time after dinner in walking about the room and thinking; now from dinner to tea-time he lay on the sofa with his face to the wall, giving himself up to trivial thoughts which he could not suppress, hard as he tried.[9]

Abandoning the only battle which would express what he is, he becomes increasingly lost in a hostile world; the chance of fulfilment once missed is not offered again. The tale contains too Chekov's answer to Tolstoy's doctrine of non-violence: he could discover no probability of reducing ignorance and barbarism by failing to fight them.

Chekov's view of the individual admits the recurrence of failure and waste. But being the least doctrinaire of writers, he does not conceive this as the result of cold and impersonal forces, which stand in the way of human endeavour, so much as the operation of life upon the individual, fashioning him in a particular way, and often rendering him impotent in relation to what he most desires. Chekov was also able to bring to most of his characters an affectionate warmth, because his observation of their failings did not destroy his sense of humour. Since he recognised so much to be immutable within the brief course of an individual life, he could only regard the discrepancy between what people wanted, and what they achieved, as finally comic. His knowledge of provincial life also sharpened his eye for the unsophisticated and ludicrous attempts which human beings make to put things to rights; and this matched a style which never became over-complex, or, in the bad sense, urbane. However brief his stories, they focus upon incidents which reveal the quality of life, and its limited possibilities at a particular moment of time.

In *Neighbours*, Peter Ivashin is exasperated because his sister has been abducted by Vlasich, a married man. Already fat and short of breath at twenty-seven, he knows he must end the stupid situation somehow or other:

> Stormy emotions raged within him. He felt the urge to do something striking and impetuous even if it meant regretting it for the rest of his life. Should he call Vlasich a blackguard, slap his face, challenge him to a duel? But Vlasich wasn't the sort who fights duels.[10]

Arriving at his neighbour's house without knowing what he is going to do, Ivashin succumbs at once to his welcome, and Vlasich's admission that he and Zina rely on his generosity. But the more Vlasich talks about his life, his debts, his house, the more Ivashin becomes convinced that the situation cannot be mended. His neighbour possesses no kind of *savoir-vivre*, and even already his sister is unhappy:

> His sister, this sensitive, elegant girl who looked so much like their mother, now lived with Vlasich and shared Vlasich's home with a

torpid maid, and six-legged table in a house where a man had been
flogged to death. And now she wouldn't be going home with her
brother, but would stay the night there. All of this struck Ivashin as
incredibly absurd.[11]

Ivashin's own growing awareness of his impotence, while it renders
even more humorous his previous rage, also underlines the story's
point about how little in human life is susceptible of change. This does
not exonerate Ivashin for not trying, as he himself knows:

> So far he had not done or said what he thought, he concluded, and
> others had repaid him in like coin, which was why all life now seemed
> as dark as this pond with its reflections of the night sky and its tangled
> water-weed.[12]

But Chekov's tone remains more lightly ironic than earnest, because
he also knows that matters cannot be mended.

Chekov's humour and his attitude to time both affect his vision of the
self. On the one hand, life is brief; everything passes, love, like life
comes to an end, chances are missed which never return. On the other
hand, nothing changes, in spite of all people hope and desire—at least
in their own lives. As a result, Chekov's characters appear to be timeless: people seen as they uniquely are, and can only be within the
limited bounds of their existence.

One of the stories most admired by Tolstoy was *The Darling*; and
it delicately hints at the reasons for which moral reformers make so
little impact on human life. Olga, the daughter of a retired civil
servant, is first married to Kukin, the proprietor of the Tivoli amuse-
ment park. Rain, or the threat of rain, causes him despair; but in spite
of the incessant downpour on his wedding day he looks at his wife and
says: 'Oh you darling!' Olga proves that she is by helping her husband
in his business, and spreading the word that only in the theatre can one
become educated and humane. But Kukin dies, and Olga falls in love
with a timber merchant, whom she marries. He prizes her no less, and
she rewards him by learning to talk about timber, completely forgetting
all she has once felt for the theatre:

> 'The price of timber, 'she would say to her acquaintances and
> customers, 'rises twenty per cent every year now. Why, we used to
> sell local timber, and now my Vasily has to go for timber to the
> Mogilyov province. And the freight!' she cried, covering her
> cheeks with her hands in horror. 'The freight!'[13]

With no opinions of her own, Olga can only live through those whom she loves; and when her third lover, a veterinary surgeon, deserts her, her life becomes as empty as her brain and her heart: 'And so it went on, day after day, year after year—no joy of any kind, and nothing to express an opinion about.'[14] Olga's character is touched by a genuine and natural affection which finally discovers an outlet in the vet's child, Sasha: 'And she would start talking about the teachers, the lessons, the school-books, repeating what Sasha had said about them. . . .'[15] Through her Chekov portrays life's ephemerality, but conceives her uniqueness so clearly that she seems to be timeless.

In three of Chekov's most famous stories, *The Butterfly*, *Ionych* and *The House with a Mezzanine*, the tragedy in the lives of individuals is perceived as the product of the interaction between their own weaknesses and time's swift passage. What might have changed them is present and gone before they can grasp it. As always in Chekov's finest work, the immediacy and openness of his style makes it easy to overlook the shaping viewpoint which lies behind. In *The Butterfly*, Olga, the wife of a junior hospital doctor, regards her husband as simple, ordinary, and undistinguished. He has no understanding of higher things, like art, whereas Olga herself has friends among the 'celebrated': painters, musicians and the like. Her husband, although knowing she deceives him and suffering from loneliness, carries on with his work at the hospital, until he catches diphtheria and dies. Only then does Olga begin to realise her husband's qualities, and to regret the time wasted with a worthless painter. As the world reminds her, she has lost her chance of finding herself in a relationship that matters. Olga's shallowness of feeling and lack of imagination are not portrayed sympathetically by Chekov; but that serves to intensify the irony of an awareness which comes too late, when time wasted cannot be redeemed.

Ionych, on the other hand, is concerned with what happens to people when they have to live with their mistakes. Dr. Startsev lives in the town of S., which possesses a number of intelligent, pleasing and interesting families, among the most prominent of whom is the Turkins. Mrs. Turkin writes novels which she reads aloud at her soirées; her daughter Kitty plays the piano abominably, and wants to be a pianist. Dr. Startsev decides to propose to her. She makes an assignation with him in the cemetery at midnight, fails to keep it, and rejects him for the music she claims to adore: 'You know that I love art more than anything in the world; I love music madly, I adore it, I want to devote my whole life to it. I want to be an artist, I want fame, success, freedom. . . .'[16] Four years later, Kitty returns to S., having discovered that she has no talent for music; she would now be glad to marry Startsev. But Startsev is no longer interested. He has acquired a large practice, grown rich, and plays bridge. He finds the people of the town uninteresting; and only his own comforts give him pleasure. The love which might have existed between them cannot be recalled: 'The days are flying and passing, life passes drearily, without impressions, without thoughts. Kitty still plays the piano, but her health is failing, and she goes to the Crimea every autumn with her mother.'[17]

Chekov's characters appear to a greater degree than Ibsen's the product of their choices; their decisions, often lightly taken, lead to more serious consequences than they could have foreseen. Chekov's irony is directed against the resulting waste; but it is tempered by his awareness of how swiftly life's opportunities disappear, and by the irrevocable consequences which flow from trivial acts. Sometimes, as in *The House with a Mezzanine*, the opposition of the stars, as much as missed opportunity, causes the lack of fulfilment, but again time only offers very fleetingly a change of potential happiness. A young land-scape painter, staying in perpetual idleness on a friend's estate, meets the Volchaninovs, who live nearby. The family consists of a mother and two daughters. The painter recognises the limitations and inadequacies of his existence. He feels pain, sadness, loneliness, and uncertainty of direction. For one night, his love for the younger sister, Zheyna, transforms his pain:

> . . . I dreamed of her as my little queen, who together with me would possess those trees, those fields, this mist, this sunset, this exquisite, wonderful countryside, in the midst of which I had felt till now so hopelessly lonely and unwanted. . . .[18]

But the following day, Zhenya has vanished for ever.

What people feel themselves to have missed forms at the centre of their lives a depressing hollow, making them appear to themselves and to others ineffectual and incomplete. The transience of opportunity also in varying degrees absolves them. Like the house itself, with its attic storey and green-shaded light, love is briefly seen, and never forgotten. While Chekov extends the interest of the story by the argument between the painter, and Lydia, the elder sister, as to the relative importance in an impoverished country of medicine and art, their debate remains a battle of words, less important than the stifled relationship. In the late plays he adds another dimension to the gentleness and discrimination with which his characters had always been portrayed, by emphasising their desire for the future to be brighter for all men than the fleeting and incomplete present, and by highlighting the courage with which they confront their contribution to that end.

In these plays, Chekov developed a style of dramatic writing that enables us to see, without being told, how distraught people are; and how hard, in spite of their ineffectualness, they try to find a way of resolving their grief. Some, like the unloved and unsuccessful Trepliev in *The Seagull*, cannot bear their inability to do so. Others, like Nina who cannot reciprocate Trepliev's love, learn through suffering 'how to endure things . . . how to bear one's cross and have faith.'[19] In the last three plays, *Uncle Vania, Three Sisters* and *The Cherry Orchard*, the most subtle and painful feelings within the characters are made clear to the audience by Chekov's artistry; and they see, sometimes with almost unbearable clarity, why things cannot be changed, however much people desire them to be. Nothing can turn Trepliev into a successful writer, or make Trigorin faithful to Nina. Chekov's art is wrought from present feeling, and is unconcerned with experiences long since passed. Lacking a historical perspective, he can concentrate on the immediate experience, and perceive its value in relation to the quality of a continuing life. The moments as they pass in Chekov's drama form a pattern of growing awareness of what each character is, and must endure—apparent to themselves, as to his audience.

The Seagull is somewhat less refined in technique than the last three plays; and because of that the theme of self-fulfilment stands out the more starkly. Inability to reciprocate love, and a lack of equivalence in people's desires, convey incompleteness. Masha is touched by Medviedenko's love, but cannot return it. Trepliev adores Nina, who does not care for him; and Masha loves Trepliev, who scarcely notices her. But the seagull symbolises another kind of frustration, and of fulfilment: that of the creative life itself. Trepliev, when he enters with the dead seagull, prophesies that he will soon kill himself; and at the play's end he does so. Thwarted in his love for Nina, he also fails to find himself as a writer; floating about in a world of dreams and images, he lacks any sense of direction, or the power to impose the new art-work of which he dreams on his audience. Poor as Trigorin's writing may be, when compared, as he compares it, with that of Dostoevsky, he is supported by fame, wealth and popularity; and short-lived as his own affections may be, he is nonetheless adored by

Nina. Trepliev does not enjoy his good fortune in love or work. He tries to fly but cannot. Nina suffers no less when Trigorin deserts her after the death of their child; but she turns her suffering to creative advantage; and while achieving scarcely more success as an actress than Trepliev does as a writer, she 'grows stronger in spirit every day'. She becomes the seagull that flies, as opposed to Trepliev's seagull that destroys itself.

Chekov portrays them both with more sympathy than Trigorin or Arkadina who, in spite of their public success, display an unchanging self-regard and lack of concern for others. All that has happened to them in the two-year interval between Acts Three and Four has left them the same. Chekov often used fixity in character for comic effect—as he does here in the case of the retired lieutenant, Shamrayev—but also to convey a humanity restricted by lack of any deep feeling. The importance of matching one's dreams to one's possibilities, and accepting the consequences, is suggested in the contrast between Nina's and Trepliev's end; but Chekov still attaches more importance to the individual who endures and searches than to the person whose experience of living does not run deep. In *The Seagull*, as in the later plays, he also uses Nature in its permanence and stillness to create a contrast with the distress of human life, and implicitly to suggest through it a beauty which human life ought to contain.

Like several of Ibsen's plays, *Uncle Vania* derives its dramatic tension from the effects of disruption upon an established way of life. The retired Professor Serebriakov and his young wife, Yeliena, return to the estate which the Professor owns; the estate is run by Vania, the brother of the Professor's first wife, and Sonia, his daughter. Vania is upset by the Professor's disturbance of their routine, by the youth and beauty of his wife, and by the fact that in spite of his eminence he is obviously a nincompoop. Vania is forty-seven, and knows that life is slipping him by, that he has achieved nothing. 'It would even be pleasant to hang oneself on a day like this,' he says. The old nurse comments, indirectly, as she feeds the chickens: 'Chook, chook, chook!'[20] All this 'pother o'er our heads' is insignificant. Vania is in love with the Professor's young wife, Yeliena (or thinks he is); Sonia loves Dr. Astrov, a regular visitor to the estate—but the doctor, through the endless monotony and fatigue of his work, has grown dead to feeling (though he too is attracted by Yeliena). All except Serebriakov sense the emptiness and incompleteness of their lives; and he has a pain

in his left leg. As Vania says to Yeliena (not without bathetic humour):
'My life, my love—look at them—where do they belong? What am
I to do with them? My feeling for you is just wasted like a ray of
sunlight falling into a well—and I am wasted too.'[21] To Yeliena this
talk of love is just stupid. Astrov's confession to Sonia is painful in a
different way:

> *Astrov*: I don't love human beings . . . I haven't cared for anyone for
> years.
> *Sonia*: Not for anyone?
> *Astrov*: No one. I feel a sort of fondness for your old nurse—for the
> sake of old times. . . .[22]

He goes on talking, but his loquacity conceals as much as Sonia's
silence. The real dialogue between them, which we can read in their
tone, expression and gesture, remains unspoken.

In Act Three, Serebriakov clumsily announces his intention of selling
the estate which Vania has looked after for so long. Vania attempts to
shoot him, and repeatedly misses. At the opposite extreme to Sonia's
stillness, Vania's frenzied excitement suggests how deeply these lives
are shaken by their desires, and the misfortunes of existence. When
finally the storm has passed, and the sound of the Professor's carriage
recedes once more from the house whose tranquillity it shattered, it
carries away Vania's love, just as Astrov's decision not to come to the
house till summer buries Sonia's. It is an ironic and painful irrelevance
that at the moment of departure Astrov should stare at the map of
Africa and remark: 'I suppose down there in Africa the heat must be
terrific now.'[23] There can be nothing more personal for them to say
to each other. But Sonia and Vania, in spite of all they suffer, and must
endure in the future, do not quite despair:

> *Sonia*: Well, what can we do? We must go on living! We shall go
> on living, Uncle Vania. We shall live through a long, long succession
> of days and tedious evenings . . . we shall work for others, now and in
> our old age, and we shall have no rest . . . Over there, beyond the
> grave . . . we shall rejoice and look back at these troubles of ours with
> tender feelings, with a smile—and we shall have rest.[24]

In these moments when Sonia has finally lost hope in the fulfilment
of her love for Astrov, she has to construct something upon which to
rejoice. However much truth we may or may not feel in Sonia's
general view of things, we cannot, after what she has suffered, doubt
either her courage or her sincerity. Sonia's sorrow belongs to a heart

that remains glad; in her hope and steadfastness she symbolises a sustained goodness at the centre of harsh and suffering existence. This is not lack of viewpoint, but a confident assertion of those values which are stronger than the arbitrariness and unhappiness of the world.

Chekov's tone has become more sombre in *Three Sisters*, the least comic and most tautly structured of his plays. In *Uncle Vania*, people are often blind to the effect of their actions, but not deliberately malicious. In *Three Sisters*, Solyony cannot accept that Irene does not love him, and even less that the Baron is his rival. In the first act he threatens to put a bullet in the Baron's head out of ill temper (a threat which is sometimes in production meaninglessly directed at Chebutykin); and in the fourth act he does so out of jealousy. Solyony, humourless and destructively mean, is only worse in degree than Natasha, the wife (after Act One) of Andrey, brother to the three sisters. Incapable of seeing how cruel she is to her husband, whom everyone knows she deceives, and to the old servant Anfisa, whom she wants turned out of the house, relentlessly and apparently unknowingly she takes over her husband's home and life, destroying him with her vulgarity, and shallowness of spirit. As Andrey is forced to admit by the end of the play, something about her 'pulls her down to the level of an animal—a sort of mean, blind, thick-skinned animal—anyway not a human being. . . .'[25] Chebutykin, one-time doctor, and now alchoholic, destroys in another way. Not having done a stroke of work since he left the university he feels that nothing is worth the effort, and that, anyway, nothing matters.[26] He makes no attempt to stop the duel between Solyony and the Baron; and when the Baron is killed, consoles himself with the newspaper: 'Let them cry for a bit. . . .'[27]

These three characters in different ways represent the negative and destructive self, incapable of looking beyond themselves for a justification of their present suffering. Work, tedious and spiritless though it may be, is seen both as a palliative for that pain, and as a hope. Vershinin exclaims: 'We've just got to work and work . . . All the happiness is reserved for our descendants, for our remote descendants.'[28] But that scarcely balances the hardship it causes in the present. Andrey finds no satisfaction in his work for the Council Office, and regrets increasingly his missed academic career. Irene, who begins with a longing for work, cannot bear what she has to do in the post office: 'It's the sort of work you do without inspiration, without even thinking. . . .'[29] Olga is worn out by her work at the school: 'Tomorrow I'm free,' she says. 'Heaven, what a joy!'[30] Masha, married to a master at the High School, is 'so bored, it's simply disgusting'.[31] In love too they are equally unhappy and unfulfilled. Masha's affair with Vershinin (himself married to a woman he finds despicable) is doomed to end when his regiment is posted away; Irene agrees to marry the Baron, admitting she does not love him, but promising to be loyal and obedient—only to have him killed in a duel by Solyony; and Andrey's love for Natasha is ended by their marriage. In such a world what people say to each other often sounds irrelevant and absurd, and their hopes for the future, whether in Moscow or lives still unborn, sound like a means of cheering themselves up. But they are not only that. In Chekov's high art the distinction between good and bad is that between those who have the faith to go on working, searching and hoping, and those who do not care, or do not think it worth the effort. His vision of reality is nourished by a belief in people who suffer and do not give up, while conscious that any rewards will not be for them to enjoy.

The Cherry Orchard (1904), Chekov's last play, expresses in its most poignant and subtle form his attitude to time. He regarded the play as a comedy, and so in the divine sense it is. What seems so important and permanent to individuals at the time, like this family's love of the cherry orchard, must inevitably undergo change. Madame Liuba cannot grasp this. Almost penniless, and compelled to sell her estate, she insists upon giving a gold coin to a passing tramp, and behaving as though the orchard is not going to be sold. Even when both silly and misguided, characters in Chekov's plays have the ability, as Liuba does, to convince one of their basic goodness. And it comes across the more strikingly for the irrelevance which threatens to overrun everything.

Act Two, in particular, impresses this upon us. The action takes place at an old wayside shrine in the country which suggests a state of limbo—the place where these people happen to be. At the opening, Charlotta, the governess, takes a shotgun off her shoulder and says thoughtfully: 'I don't know how old I am. I haven't got a proper identity-card, you see.'[32] Later Lopakhin, destined to buy the estate, reminds Liuba and Gayev: 'We must decide once and for all: time won't wait. . . .'[33] But in limbo time doesn't exist: 'Who's been smoking such abominable cigars here?'[34] Liuba asks in reply to Lopakhin, and goes on to admit how senselessly, recklessly she is spending her money. Lopakhin complains that they don't seem to understand the estate is up for sale, Liuba asks, 'What are we to do? Tell us, what?'[35] They way of life they have always known will never be changed, and disappear; and Trofimov, the eternal student, will always be present to comfort as well as chide them: 'The whole of Russia is our orchard. The earth is great and beautiful, and there are many, many wonderful places on it.'[36] In a world so entrenched in a sense of its permanence, the remote sound of a string, snapping—perhaps a cable in one of the mines—causes the most disturbance. Like the Serebriakovs, though far less obtrusively, it suggests the raid of time upon stillness. In that stillness the voices of the unfulfilled—Sonia, Anya, Liuba, Gayev—desirous, if not capable, of faring forward, are heard. Like the cherry orchard itself, time overtakes them; but not before their uniqueness and the 'ground of their beseeching' has been portrayed with all the fineness and subtlety of Chekov's art. The cherry orchard is an image of great beauty: doomed to be cut down, but remaining memorable as something which Time cannot change or touch. The curtain of the theatre itself discovers it every time that it rises: 'It is May, but in the orchard there is morning frost. . . .'[37]

Chekov is like Hardy in that his mastery comes from a quality perceived within people. Without Hardy's elaborate stage-setting, his characters appear to us more directly as 'only undefeated because they have gone on trying'. Both through his work as a doctor and through his imagination, Chekov knew how much poverty, boredom and indifference worsened the quality of people's lives. His art, in its content and formal beauty, speaks quietly and resiliently against such things; and the brighter future for which his characters work and hope expresses the nature of their particular quests. Time and circumstance operate against their chance of fulfilment. While recognising the amount of waste in all existence, Chekov celebrated its goodness, not only in what people are, but in what they intend.

8

E. M. FORSTER

The armour of falsehood is subtly wrought out of darkness, and hides man not only from others, but from his own soul.
A Room with a View (1908)

E. M. Forster was born in 1879, and published his first novel, *Where Angels Fear to Tread*, at the age of twenty-six. Although he grew up in the nineties, he never showed any liking for aestheticism; and his personal vision, when formed, showed a passion for seriousness and truth which gave him his place among the writers of the new century, not with the last of the old. His finest work was to be done in the 'vestibule' to what he later described as 'the sinister corridor of our age'. In his second year at Cambridge he ceased to believe in Christianity: '. . . I never had much sense of sin and when I realised that the main aim of the Incarnation was not to stop war or pain or poverty, but to free us from sin I became less interested and ended by scrapping it too. . . .'[1] Forster described this as the first grand 'discovery' of his youth; he always remained a writer committed to the values which exist this side of the grave. Of equal importance to him—and the second 'grand discovery' of his youth—was his awakening to the greatness of the world, in which his relationship with H. O. Meredith played an important part. For Forster the fullest expression of humanity could only occur when the inner life was not impoverished by convention or prejudice, and the self discovered through relationships with others. Like Chekov, he did not belong to the modern world—clearly though he recognised its necessary evolution. He saw its gathering complexities from a standpoint of deep personal conviction no longer possible after the catastrophe of the First World War; and he belonged to a social environment which owed its values to a long and cherished past. The kind of civilisation for which Forster stood was exactly that which lost a great deal of its authority in the years between 1914 and 1918: those writers who subsequently wished to ascribe as much value as he did to private worlds were compelled to discover more oblique and wayward means of expressing them.

Perhaps because this was already so, Forster's place in literary achievement seems somewhat less considerable than the writers already discussed. His characters appear too much the product of their narrow social environment to achieve that fully detachable humanity and representativeness characteristic of Mann or Hardy. Real as Forster's characters are, they belong to their period; and cannot be thought of without some reference to it. Forster's novels portray middle-class life in the years before the war. They are deft in their eye and ear for social nuance, acute in their evocation of family life in particular places, and sharply accurate in their detection of flaws in feeling.

But Forster's stature as an artist derives from the personal vision which gives tone and originality to such portraiture. Whether writing of England, Italy, or finally India, he was concerned with the ways in which the potential in individual life could be ruined or realised, and with the forces, whether public or private, involved in this process. Unlike Chekov, Forster allowed most of his major characters the opportunity to grasp what life offered them, if only they freed themselves from muddle, and were true to their real selves. Although death often comes unexpectedly and at untimely moments in his fiction, the serious business of living still involves choices; and the nature of these choices is significant both for the individual and for their influence upon the lives of others. Time moves more slowly than in Chekov's works; and this permits a more optimistic account of the possibilities which the individual can fulfil. Unlike Ibsen, on the other hand, Forster does not conceive of the process of becoming what one is in isolation from others, but in relationships with them. His celebration of life is always a shared experience.

The earliest of the novels, *Where Angels Fear to Tread* (1905) is a gracefully ironic social comedy, which at once establishes Forster's powers of combining levity and seriousness. In spite of its recurrent deaths, among which that of Gino's child is certainly tragic, the novel views with a humorous eye the lives and manners of the English middle classes as they come into contact with the darker and more saturnine powers of Italy. At the same time Forster quickly establishes his dislikes: prejudice, snobbery, lack of any deep feeling. He depicts Mrs. Herriton as a woman who remains able to think well of herself, even when her acts show no understanding of, or respect for, the different needs of others; and her possessiveness as an aspect of her conviction of national and class superiority. Forster never had any liking for either.

Like all important writers of fiction, he also instinctively knows how to make powerful instruments out of the simplest objects—as, for example, the picture postcards sent from Italy which make Irma Herriton aware of the existence of her half-brother in Italy, and reveal Mrs. Herriton's calculating coldness in relation to the boy. Money, she believes, will be quite sufficient to persuade his father to give him up for ever; and adoption the means of providing the English upbringing he requires. Her calculating manner of expressing feeling is contrasted with the Italian passion which Gino, for all his faults, feels for his son: instinctive, unreflective and profound. Forster's success with differences in orientation of feeling is marked: the individual does not become submerged in the national type; rather, through the individual he makes us aware of central differences in temperament; and these are used to create the mounting tension within the novel.

A writer of fiction, attempting to create foreign characters, must always surmount the difficulty of their sounding, for example, like Italianate Englishmen; and Forster's ear for subtleties in dialogue, as well as his acute observation of modes of behaviour, proves admirably equipped for the task. Gino does not speak like an Englishman; but he also does not sound as though he is being translated:

All Gino cared about at present was idleness and pocket-money; and his way of expressing it was to exclaim: 'Ouf-pouf! How hot it is in here. No air; I sweat all over. I expire. I must cool myself, or I shall never get to sleep!'[2]

Whether in the opera house at Monteriano, or in the drawing room at Sawston, Forster hears and watches how people behave with a shrewdness that reveals their inner personality. The artistry of the external social observation makes possible the expression of the deeper commitment to inner being; and it is this which gives the novel its distinct originality. Without the recognition of the need for inner truth, *Where Angels Fear to Tread* would have remained a graceful and somewhat melodramatic tale, of period interest only. As it is, the possibility of achieving self-realisation emerges out of the novel's subtle and acute organisation as the central theme: not as something imposed, but as the natural and controlling emphasis of the story.

When Caroline Abbott returns to Italy to try to undo the evil which she feels she assisted by conniving at Lilia's fatal marriage to Gino, she has no notion that 'wicked' people can be capable of love. Only the sight of Gino with his child brings about a change in her heart, and makes her realise how love is more important than duty. What she now feels for Gino alters also the manner in which she sees Philip Herriton. Unable to take any action without wiring home to his mother for instructions, he reveals the extent of his deadness: nothing happens to him inside. Or it has not, until he is 'saved' by becoming aware of his love for Charlotte Abbott: 'He had reached love by the spiritual path: her thoughts and her goodness and her nobility had moved him first, and now her whole body and all its gestures had become transfigured by them.'[3] That his love will not be reciprocated matters less than its effect upon him. Deciding to free himself from his mother's domination and to leave home, he will be able to 'go among people who may hope to understand him'. Even now, understanding the passion which has awakened him, he can rejoice in all that has been good in the experience they have shared in Italy:

> This episode which she thought so sordid, and which was so tragic for him, remained supremely beautiful. To such a height was he lifted, that without regret he could now have told her that he was her worshipper too. But what was the use of telling her? For all the wonderful things that had happened.[4]

The novel's end celebrates a new degree of awareness in Charlotte Abbott and Philip Herriton: their humanity has been enlarged by the experiences through which they have passed; and they themselves have discovered, in spite of their suffering, more of the greatness of the world. And yet in this short novel, the final transformations are too cursorily treated for a detailed investigation of their nature to be possible. What permanent effect they will have upon the life of Philip, in particular, even if he does break away from Sawston and his mother, remains an open question. In *The Longest Journey*, which Forster had begun before *Where Angels Fear to Tread*, he took a more distanced and perspective view of the importance he attached to the inner life, and gave to the figure of Rickie Elliott a centrality which no one character had possessed in the more highly contrived earlier novel. It is not difficult to see why *The Longest Journey* retained a high place in Forster's affections.

The novel is concerned with the failure of a young man, Rickie Elliott, to become an artist—with his 'spiritual ruin', and partial regeneration, before his early death. In the civilised Cambridge world, where the novel opens, Rickie and his friends discuss the philosophic problem of whether a cow exists only when there is someone to see it;

and Forster makes it suggest the more imponderable mystery of what is real for the individual, and how he keeps that image alive. For the young Rickie Elliott who wishes to be a writer, 'elms can be dryads', and a dell near Cambridge a church 'where indeed you could do anything you liked, but where anything you did would be transfigured'.[5] This power to transfigure reveals in Rickie an active imagination, of which the danger consists in his tendency to confuse his imaginings with a realistic assessment of what life is like. While Rickie confines himself to writing stories about pagan gods (which may or may not be good) his imagination is working in its proper sphere; but when he allows it to affect his view of Agnes Pembroke, after the sudden death of her fiancé, he starts to expose himself to a more threatening situation: 'And so Rickie deflected his enthusiasms. Hitherto they had played on gods and heroes, on the infinite and impossible, on virtue and beauty and strength. Now with a steadier radiance, they transfigured a man who was dead and a woman who was still alive.'[6] Agnes, whose real life comes to an end with the death of Gerald, settles for a marriage with Rickie; and he, seeing her only in her relation to Gerald, fails to perceive the threat she is to his real self. Unimaginative, conventional, snobbish, greedy and impoverished, Agnes lacks understanding of why Rickie's stories are important to him, and the values necessary to him if he is to continue to write. Rickie's Cambridge friend, Ansell, sees at once the impending disaster: 'She is happy because she has conquered; he is happy because he has at last hung all the world's beauty on to a single peg. . . .'[7]

Forster's analysis of Rickie's life depends on the idea of the 'symbolic moment'. Such a moment occurs when Rickie fails to acknowledge his half-brother, Stephen Wonham, for motives inspired by his wife's greed and sense of class. Rickie knows that he is failing to be true to himself, but he lacks the strength to resist Agnes, who fears to lose 'what has been comfortably arranged'. The best he can do is try to explain:

It seems to me that here and there in life we meet with a person or incident that is symbolical. It's nothing in itself, yet for the moment it stands for some eternal principle. We accept it, at whatever cost, and we have accepted life. But if we are frightened and reject it, the moment so to speak passes; the symbol is never offered again.[8]

This idea of the symbolic moment reflects Forster's concern with seriousness and truth: the view that if the individual is to survive he has to remain true to those things which are the expression of his own real nature. Character reveals its quality by reference to this standard. Ansell's anger and disappointment with Rickie over his marriage may indicate jealousy; but more importantly, it voices a commentary upon what is happening to Rickie within. Rickie rejects the symbolic moment, suffers a curious breakdown, and discovers that 'some imperceptible bloom had passed from the world'.[9] He no longer takes such acute pleasure in people, and his writing loses its early promise. Isolated from his friends by Agnes, and cut off from the springs of his talent, he begins to live in a world of unreality, in which he feels that 'the cow was not really there'.[10] In abandoning the quest for self, Rickie ensures that the spiritual part of him proceeds towards ruin.

There are not many novels (Turgenev's *Smoke* is another example) which succeed in working out the implications of an idea without losing their grasp of individualised character, and at the same time conveying the importance of the idea in itself. Forster achieves this in *The Longest Journey*, but at the cost of some indistinctness in the presentation of the other characters. Rickie's mother, the Pembrokes, Mrs. Failing, all lack that fully rounded articulation which he was to achieve with the characters of his next novel, *A Room with a View*. Their voices come from a distance, compared with the central voice telling of Rickie's spiritual journey. Even the unfettered and uncontrollable instincts in Stephen Wonham, Rickie's half-brother, seem less thoroughly assimilated within his English temperament than in the case of the Italian Gino. Forster was never entirely at ease when writing of the English who were not 'gentle-folk'.

Although Rickie's desire to be a writer remains a central aspect of his personality, and Forster depicts him as returning to his writing when he abandons his destructive marriage, the value attached to art is significantly less than that attributed to the relationships between people for their own sake—not for some value he thinks they represent. In spite of the difficulty of believing in Stephen, or even finding him likeable, Rickie loses his life trying to pull him off the railway line when drunk. The act symbolises that necessity in individuals which they can only deny in themselves at the cost of the inner life: a price which renders life empty and sterile. The holiness of the heart's affections, and the responsibility they involve outside the conventions which limit and cripple them, are of central importance in Forster's view of things. Rickie's failure to be true to himself stultifies his life as an artist; but that matters less than his impoverishment as a human being. The quest for self is bound up with the ability to love; and that ability is the only kind of religion the book accepts.

In *A Room with a View* (1908) Forster combines the depth of vision of *The Longest Journey* with the shrewd social comedy of *Where Angels Fear to Tread*; and his style is marked by a subtle and delicate precision. Once again the façade of the novel is constructed from a temperately ironic view of middle-class life; but its inner passion derives from a concern that people should not destroy themselves, and those with whom they come into contact, by failing to recognise what matters in their lives. Here it is Lucy Honeychurch, who is pulled back from disaster by the father of the man she finally marries. Armed with clear self-knowledge, Mr. Emerson is also able to see where the truth lies for Lucy and help her to understand it. Lucy suffers from muddle within, and about herself, which Mr. Emerson knows to be dangerous:

Take an old man's word: there's nothing worse than a muddle in all the world. It is easy to face Death and Fate, and the things that sound so dreadful. It is on my muddles that I look back with horror—on the things that I might have avoided. We can help one another but little. I used to think I could teach young people the whole of life, but I know better now, and all my teaching of George has come down to this: beware of muddle.[11]

Mr. Emerson's attack on muddle formulates in an exact way a more general preoccupation of the novel. The avoidance of catastrophe does not depend upon the achievement of a new level of enlightenment as it does, for example, in T. S. Eliot's plays, but upon not succumbing to a rigidity of view that obstructs development. Cecil Vyse, to whom Lucy is for a time engaged, is interested in books, art and music in a manner that precludes intimacy with other people. This emotional restriction in his personality, whether or not he is to be blamed for it, makes him a lesser human being because it involves living vicariously through things; it precludes that full participation in living, through which the self is understood, strengthened and developed. At another level, the disapproval of Mr. Eager for the innocent amorousness of the Italian couple who drive the English to Fiesole, and the more sinister rejection by Mr. Beebe of the engagement between Lucy and George, at the end of the novel, suggestively extend the same theme. Miss Bartlett, Lucy's companion on the trip to Italy, is let off more lightly and also more ambiguously by Forster; she appears in the course of the novel to lack insight into the nature of Lucy's problems, and even to

E

resist her natural development. But in the final page of the book, Forster allows the possibility 'that far down in her heart, far below all speech and behaviour, she is glad.'[12]

The novel differs from the two previous works in its ability not merely to celebrate final recognitions, but to derive from the process of life an elation that is vivid and effective. The violets among which George and Lucy first kiss are invested with mystery and joy:

> From her feet the ground sloped sharply into the view, and violets ran down in rivulets, and streams and cataracts, irrigating the hill-side with blue, eddying round the tree-stems, collecting into pools in the hollows, covering the grass with spots of azure foam. . . .[13]

Much later in the novel, when Freddy takes George and Mr. Beebe swimming, the pool becomes a 'momentary chalice for youth'.[14] Instinctive and unfettered delight overcomes their normally inhibited natures. Such moments pass—and not without humour—but their 'passing benediction' leaves its imprint on the novel as a whole.

Forster succeeds too in portraying with more generosity than in *Where Angels Fear to Tread* the life of an English country house: not grand, but comfortable and apparently secure in its assumptions. Windy Corner possesses the strengths and limitations of life worn smooth by long-established conventions. It offers little inducement to the inhabitants to possess their own soul; and it is this which Italy has unconsciously offered to Lucy. Windy Corner threatens to stifle her again, confusing the real issues and muddying with its moderate temper the nature of the choices:

> The contest lay not between love and duty. Perhaps there is never such a contest. It lay between the real and the pretended, and Lucy's first aim was to defeat herself.[15]

She attempts to do this by tampering with the truth. Rejecting Cecil because she realises the impossibility of marrying him, she also has to deny the existence of her love for George:

> She gave up trying to understand herself, and joined the vast armies of the benighted, who follow neither the heart nor the brain, and mark their destiny by catchwords. The armies are full of pleasant and pious folk. But they have yielded to the only enemy that matters—the enemy within.[16]

Lucy's flight from self-knowledge is precipitous; and only Mr. Emerson's perceptiveness, matched by a practical ability to deal with the crises of life, prevents her from proceeding to ruin. While Lucy is committing suicide through abandoning the quest for self-knowledge, George has succumbed to despair—the disease of thinking it not worth while to live. Unlike the two clergymen in the novel, Mr. Emerson is presented as being profoundly religious. Because he is true to himself, and to the practice of love which in his own way he represents, he is able to respect life and affirm its value. He knows that all men and women have souls which they can ruin; and if they do so, through failing to understand themselves, they are lost. What he gives Lucy in passionately persuading her to marry George is 'a sense of the deities reconciled, a feeling that in gaining the man she loved, she would gain something for the whole world'.[17]

A Room with a View is touched with that Italian sunlight in which, as Forster said, people learn to say yes. Forster always attended to the implications of what his characters said and did: his comments, both shrewd and meditated, play an important part in the book's effectiveness. But finally what people feel when their lives are not stultified by rigidity or convention emerges as the most important concern. Through the achievement of love and happiness, life becomes a celebratory act. In their acceptance or rejection of the passion and truth in themselves, men and women make their choice between life and death. For Forster, the implications of this are wider than individual happiness or fulfilment. Only those who do not deny the life within them are capable of love; and only through love, human and ephemeral as it is, can the better world, in which Mr. Emerson believes, come into existence.

With *Howards End* (1910) Forster extended the scope and comprehensiveness of his fiction. While the earlier novels said much about the quality—and the limitations—of English life, *Howards End* attempted to say more about its direction and movement. Implicit in the novel is the view that the way of life it describes is changing fast, and will soon disappear in the encroaching greyness of London. But Forster did not attempt, as Wells and Shaw did, to prophesy the shape of things to come, or to conceive how the old order would be changed by the new. Rather the novel expressed a scepticism about the modern world of spreading suburbia, and the proliferation of the motor car. It extended a good deal of sympathy for life at Howards End. The 'millionaire' Mr. Wilcox, for all his defects of imagination, remains likeable, while the oppressed and impoverished clerk, Leonard Bast, never appears so—not least because he is portrayed as being pathetically

ill-equipped to cope with life. His heart-attack, which causes Charles
Wilcox to be sent to prison on a charge of manslaughter, seems but the
final manifestation of his irritating incompetence. Forster believed that
the future belonged to some form of socialism; but his emotional
sympathies remained with that old world where the individual counted
for more than any collective ideal.

Howards End is given its firm and clear structure by preoccupations
which are not in origin social at all. Once again, Forster has in mind a
distinction between those who get themselves right, and those who do
not. At the climax of the novel, Margaret Wilcox confronts her
husband with his condemnation of her sister for becoming pregnant
outside marriage, while forgetting his infidelity to his first wife:

> You shall see the connection if it kills you, Henry! You have had a
> mistress—I forgave you. My sister has a lover—you drive her from
> the house. Do you see the connection? Stupid, hypocritical, cruel—
> oh contemptible—a man who insults his wife, when she alone, and
> cants with her memory when she's dead . . . I've spoilt you long
> enough. All your life you've been spoiled. No one has ever told you
> what you are—muddled, criminally muddled.[18]

The estrangement which arises between the Wilcoxes out of this muddle
is only healed when Charles's conviction causes Mr. Wilcox's collapse,
and Margaret takes him down to Howards End 'to recruit'. Her action
is symbolic in two ways. It suggests her knowledge of where insistence
upon her point no longer has relevance; and it reaffirms the value of
Howards End as a place where acceptance of life's terms becomes
possible.

But the spiritual values associated with Howards End have little
relevance in the changing world beyond. Margaret Schlegel, Mrs.
Wilcox's spiritual heir, admits her awareness early in the novel of the
dependance of civilisation on money. Mrs. Wilcox would not have
discussed such things; and though the gradation of change is small,
exactly that change in awareness threatens the Howards End way of
life, as it actually destroys Margaret's home in Wickham Place, so
that the landlord may obtain more rent by building flats. Like the earlier
novels, *Howards End* communicates the view that 'private life holds out
the mirror to infinity'—but by seeing the environment in which that
private life is conducted as threatened by change in social attitudes and
activity, the novel expresses doubt as to what the future for the private
life will hold. It is significant that the Wilcox children could not be

imagined as inhabiting Howards End, and that Charles and Dolly's own house reflects a more modern insistence on material comfort. Conversely, Margaret's sister, Helen, who desires to redress the balance of injustice and inequality in the old world, only comes to accept Howards End when the complexity of the problems she has thrown herself into forces her back to it, rebuffed. But Helen also represents a variation on a theme with which Forster had long been preoccupied. Helen lacks any real inner life of her own; and because she does, she proves impotent and destructive in relation to others. Her dislikes are well enough founded, but her manner of attempting to deal with them crude and false. Only when rid of the hatred which reflects her own lack of fulfilment can she begin to be constructive in her attitude towards others. At Howards End she starts to accept herself and her limitations, which enables her also to discover the meaning of love.

In *Howards End*, Forster succeeds better than ever before in making locality serve the end of defining his vision. London, Shropshire, Dorset, Hertfordshire are used as the various settings for Margaret Schlegel's slow movement towards finding herself, and her position in life: a position which is creative in relation to others, because it expresses what she is, and she can accept it. The two Mrs. Wilcoxes mark the difference between a world in which assurance comes naturally, and one in which it only exists through the increasingly fine definition of character. The first Mrs. Wilcox lives in the seclusion of her family and home; she admits that if Howards End had been pulled down, it would have killed her. It is only when speaking of her house that her rather expressionless voice quickens. At Margaret Schlegel's lunch-party she is dismissed as being uninteresting; she has no conversation to amuse, no interest in the topics of the day. But Mrs. Wilcox has a spiritual life of her own: private, inviolate and which centres upon Howards End, the house with its nine windows, its wych-elm and its vine. She combines a desire not to vex people with an understanding of what must be done in moments of crisis. It is thus that she first appears:

> She seemed to belong not to the young people and their motor, but to the house, and to the tree that overshadowed it. One knew that she worshipped the past, and that the instinctive wisdom the past can alone bestow had descended upon her—that wisdom to which we give the clumsy name of aristocracy.[19]

Mrs. Wilcox is depicted as being without bitterness, and without criticism—but also out of focus with daily life. Her detachment makes possible her 'delicate imaginings', and her ability to help others in her way.

Margaret Schlegel is not permitted that degree of detachment; her focus on daily life has been sharpened by her German background, her assumption of responsibility for the Schlegel family at an early age, and her participation in a social milieu where people think. She belongs to that more complex modern world which is being created, where assurance does not come easily, and delicate imaginings are easily and frequently assaulted. Forster's success with her consists in the way he suggests—much more subtly than in the case of the first Mrs. Wilcox—that her private world is preserved unharmed. She does not go wrong in her dealings with people, as Helen does; and she finds herself finally in her love for Mr. Wilcox:

> To have no illusions, and yet to love—what stronger surety can a woman find? She had seen her husband's past as well as his heart. She knew her own heart with a thoroughness that common-place people believe impossible.[20]

Knowing herself, she can also recognise how important her husband's self-deception is. Such knowledge, preserved against the muddles and confusion in the world, is something won for the future; and like the house, it exists above the materialism which threatens to destroy it.

The conclusion of *Howards End* displays Forster's mastery of style at its finest. The continuing life of the old country house mirrors Margaret Schlegel's ability to accept and endure in a manner that creates peace for others: an evenness of temperament only to be achieved through truth to self:

> Fourteen months had passed, but Margaret still stopped at Howards End. No better plan had occurred to her. The meadow was being recut, the great red poppies were reopening in the garden. July would follow with the little red poppies among the wheat, August with the cutting of the wheat. These little events would become part of her year after year.[21]

As in the year, so in her life at Howards End a sense of proportion exists which enables love to survive. Based upon the discovery and acceptance of the role each individual must play, it acts as a safeguard against the confusion of the outside world; and it also makes possible a perception of the realities which lie beyond the pressures of everyday life.

A Passage to India extends the horizons of Forster's fiction from the national to the racial and cultural. Inevitably, the larger framework tends to diminish the importance of individual fulfilment—by alteration of perspective, if nothing else. It also dimmed the positive emphasis of the personal vision, showing more in the human situation as being incapable of any solution within the lifetime of the characters concerned. Mrs. Moore dies at sea, weary of the human voices quarrelling around her, and unable to make sense of her experience; the 'Boum' of the Marabar caves, however interpreted, does not provide any clarification of the confusion she feels surrounding her existence. The friendship which potentially exists between Aziz and Fielding has no future until the British are driven out of India; and the differences between Hindu and Moslem remain as sharp as ever, in spite of a temporary 'entente'.

A Passage to India was started before the First World War as a result of Forster's visit to India in 1912, and completed after his second visit in 1921-2. The novel was influenced by the changed tone of the relationship which resulted from the increasing insistence upon independence, and events as sinister as the Amritsar massacre. But the social ambiance of Chandrapore, its attitudes and conventions, belong to an Edwardian fiction, basically unchallenged by the threat of immediate and sweeping change. We might then wish to see Forster's India as properly mythical: a manner of conceiving the inability of men to love one another, and of the difficulties which obstruct the growth of understanding between people of different nations and creeds. But the novel does not succeed in developing this kind of mythical power, because Forster rightly presents the Raj as being a local and passing event, rooted to the point of caricature in English modes of thought and behaviour. The dialogue too, of which Forster here, as always, proves a master, has the accent and idiosyncrasy of an extremely provincial environment. It is no more capable of suggesting a universally representative fiction than Chekov's town of S. in *Ionych*. And yet the fiction, by the immensity of the stage on which it is set, contains intimations of a larger concept.

The three-part form of the novel—'Mosque', 'Caves' and 'Temple' —reflects the antiquity and randomness of India itself; it also embodies aspects of Forster's preoccupation with the individual's attempts, whether successful or not, to free himself from muddle and enter into real relationships with others. The English colonists in the novel (with the exception of Fielding) manifest a rigidity of temperament that permits of no development. With their conviction of being right, and their frenzied hysteria when they feel anyone to be letting the side down, the English in India have given up the struggle through which significant human relationships are developed. Their reactions more resemble those of puppets than people, performing, like Mrs. Herriton and the Pembrokes, according to the manner in which they have been conditioned. In Fielding, Forster represents that liberal and imaginative humanism which is capable of resisting prejudice and injustice, but remains vulnerable because of an essential 'niceness'. Miss Quested herself is conceived as another of those characters, like Rickie Elliott and Lucy Honeychurch, who nearly come to disaster; but in her case the consequences of self-deception are proportionately more significant in the extent of their repercussions. The damage caused to the relationships between the communities by Miss Quested's false accusation will not be healed; and Aziz's own life will be haunted by his persecution until the British are driven out of India.

Nowhere does Forster state more clearly the importance of realising the truth about ourselves; and yet Miss Quested's case is represented as being more shadowy than the rest. Forster was coming close to that view of human character in which the individual may be powerless to control the less conscious impulses which work against human good. Miss Quested is set round by fears that play upon her doubt as to what actually happened, not least her fears about her impending marriage to Ronnie. She suffers a nervous breakdown; and in doing so reveals her inability to cope with the complexities of the situation with which India has confronted her. Miss Quested's case is less penetrable than that of Lucy Honeychurch; but she is still given the strength to save herself in the court-room. Her withdrawal of the charge against Aziz, although it cannot repair the damage already done, saves her at least from the lie in her own soul, and enables her to participate again in normal human relationships.

In the public world too, although the novel is pervaded by many misgivings, it does not despair of the future, or of some of the legacy from the past. Even though Aziz cannot conceive of friendship with the English now, he can conceive of it in the future. And in spite of the immediate political hostility, hatred remains a less powerful emotion than the love aroused in Aziz's mind by the memory of Mrs. Moore. In their own way, Godbole's ceremonies also bear witness to the presence of this positive force: 'The festival flowed on, wild and sincere, and all men loved each other, and avoided by instinct whatever caused inconvenience or pain.'[22] Forster, unlike the writers of the next section, did not consider that there was any obvious way of alleviating the human condition. Even the most absolutely held values become relative against the background of India. But his work celebrates the possibility of avoiding catastrophe, and of redeeming something from the muddle of human affairs, when the individual remains true to his own developing self. Forster conceived that as possible only in the continuing commitment of relationship to others.

Part Four: new worlds for old

When a metaphysical system, when a religion, when a great philosophy disappears from humanity, it is perhaps far more humanity itself which disappears from this philosophy . . . it is we who die away. . . .
Charles Péguy

9

CHARLES PÉGUY

George Bernard Shaw was exaggerating when he complained that in the last part of the nineteenth century civilisation had been going to the devil because mind, will and purpose had been banished from the universe. And yet he was not wholly misrepresenting a commonly held belief about the probable effects of science and materialism on contemporary society. Among the braver spirits, the failure of old beliefs led to a search for new ones, and the conviction that the hope for Man in the future lay in his development of higher intelligence, and the elimination of poverty and injustice. If this was the only world in which to believe (and there existed no future and happier state to look forward to as palliative or compensation) then man must himself evolve into a more effective, rational and humane being—or, without the props of a morality decreed by God, decline into anarchy and confusion. Among writers who shared this outlook, art became an inquiry into a man's role as a social being, and the means of improving society. The three writers to be considered now all attempted to find a solution to the problems of the modern world, and its lack of positive beliefs, by social and political commitment. Or this at least was their starting-point, for all three also found it necessary to build upon this foundation a personal vision of the future which gave social progress a particular objective, and prevented political activity from being only a struggle for power between individuals and nations. They were all idealists; and both their strengths and their limitations arise from this fact.

Shaw and Wells, in particular, are difficult territory for the literary critic. Because they deal in ideas, their verbal artistry lacks the complexity and emotional depth of writers like Hardy and Conrad. They require less interpretation because, although they may appear to contradict themselves in different works, their meaning in particular ones is seldom in doubt. In their novels and plays they illustrated the waste of the present, which appalled their moral sense, and attempted to see how in the future a harsh struggle for existence could be replaced by a more humane, just and intelligent organisation of human affairs. Their art sprang from a conviction that man needed something to steer by, and that he had lost a sense of what this could be. While their writing did not overcome the problem of trying to foresee what the future would hold, it combined a buoyant investigation of contemporary ills with an attempt to consider how they might be removed. This resulted in an art thinner in texture than that of their contemporaries—but they did succeed, as Tolstoy had not, in modifying the forms of fiction and drama to make them the instruments for what they wanted to say. Charles Péguy is a writer of another kind altogether; sharing the same view of the necessary goal, he nevertheless came to different conclusions as to the possible means. He serves to illustrate the case of the writer who tried to combine the social awareness which was beginning to transform the life of Europe with beliefs that derived from the European past.

The background to the art of Charles Péguy requires some introduction, since the conflict between science and traditional values in the later part of the century took a somewhat different form in France to that in England. This was scarcely surprising. The Revolution of 1789 had already had a profound effect on French thought and life. To the nation which had deified Reason, the attractions of science, both pure and applied, were obvious enough. At a time when the value of scientific theory was still being keenly debated in England, Auguste Comte had already constructed a scientific account of the development of human thought; Hippolyte Taine was attempting an explanation of literature, and of historical facts, in terms of race, environment, and time; while Ernest Renan, among the most promising theologians of his day, had renounced the Catholic Church out of determination to rid the world of supernaturalism. The influence of these three men on French thought in the late nineteenth century was prestigious; and each in his way contributed to the advance of science as a new kind of orthodoxy. Paul Claudel was later to speak of those 'sad years of the eighties' in which 'everything of importance, in art, in science, and in literature was irreligious.' It was against this environment, and the analytical methods on which it was based, that the symbolist poets were to show so pronounced and fierce a reaction. Maurice Maeterlinck, in his *Treasury of the Humble* (1897), exulted in the fact that 'a spiritual epoch is perhaps upon us.' The manifestations of the soul were, in his view, 'everywhere', and 'they were strangely urgent, pressing, imperious even, as though the order had been given, and no time must be lost.'[1] From a later viewpoint in time, some of these manifestations of the spirit may seem less interesting than they were thought to be then. Spirituality, when not supported by some rigorous system of thought, soon loses its bloom.

Charles Péguy, as playwright and essayist, stands between the scientific-rationalist tradition which dominated the eighties and the symbolist movement which expressed so sharp a reaction against it. Although greatly influenced by the disciplines of rational and analytic inquiry, he was not in the end a rationalist. No materialist philosophy contented him; but equally a symbolism unrelated to the socialist cause could never have satisfied his political fervour.

Charles Péguy was born in 1873, the son of a carpenter in Orléans who died when his son was only a few months old. Brought up by his mother and grandmother, he was deeply proud of his peasant blood, and the values of honesty and hard work which he saw the peasants as representing in the world before 1880. (This in itself provides an interesting contrast with Chekov's view of the Russian peasants.) While his mother saved the family from financial disaster by her practical skills, his grandmother gave him the earliest elements of his education. He commemorated this in his dedication to one of his most famous poems, 'Le Chanson du Roi Dagobert':

> À la mémoire de ma grandmère,
>   paysanne,
> qui ne savait pas lire
> et qui première m'enseigna
> le langage français.*[2]

He was destined to become the first literate member of his family.

At school his intellectual ability soon manifested itself: he took to learning with that 'concentration, seriousness and industry' which was to characterise his life, and which he owed in part to the traditions of his family. By 1894 Péguy had won his way to the École Normale Supérieure; and had absorbed the two most important influences upon his future life. He had become a convinced socialist, and he had begun to gather notes for his play on Joan of Arc. By the previous year he had already lost his faith, and declared himself a self-styled atheist

---

* 'To the memory of my peasant grandmother, who did not know how to read, and who first taught me the French language.'

who 'believed in the possibility of human brotherhood.' Socialism to him was not simply a political philosophy, but a new way of life which he believed human beings could, and should, attain. The value attached to the pursuit of money in contemporary society, and the resulting depreciation of the value of labour in, and for, itself, had in his view degraded human relationships. In addition, the economic oppression of a capitalist society debased them further by permitting some to live in a state of 'misery' (he distinguished between this and poverty which, as in the case of the peasants, was not necessarily a dishonourable and dis-honouring condition). Socialism provided an answer to economic oppression; but it also expressed the concepts of justice and charity on which he believed a human society ought to be based. His political ideas were not only directed to the relief of human ills (although he had a direct experience of those from the poverty of his childhood) but to fashioning a Christian city on earth.

Péguy's complex personality was dominated by his atheistic socialism, and his obsessive imaginative interest in Joan of Arc. Orléans, as his childhood home, remained close to Péguy's affections, and Joan as its patron saint was naturally meaningful to him. Joan's own simple origins, and her burning faith in the rightness of her cause, made her additionally sympathetic to Péguy. What the foreign conqueror was to Joan, Péguy perceived too in the form of greed and materialism which threatened France. The voices which Joan heard, Péguy wished every Frenchman to hear in uniting to build the socialist city. But his sense of affinity with Joan came too from her suffering; and in the pain which she had to endure to find her own way.

Péguy's life was shaped by his decision to abandon the possibility of a distinguished academic career at the Sorbonne. With the little money his wife had been left in a legacy, he founded a socialist library, and started the publication of *Les Cahiers de la Quinzaine*, a literary and political review in which his own works were later to appear; as well as being a poet and playwright, Péguy remained a polemicist for the socialist cause as he saw it. Like Ruskin and Carlyle, he believed deeply in the value and dignity of human labour; but the value of labour could not be assessed in relation to its earning-power. This derived from its contribution to the human brotherhood in which all should share equally, and where no work honestly and sincerely done could be regarded as more important than any other. Péguy's life and work was dedicated not to the way things are, but to the way they should be;

and like all men of his kind, he chose an isolated and stony path.

Péguy's French intellectual temperament demanded absolute loyalty from his followers, who never numbered many. His ardent and self-sacrificing nature inspired admiration and friendship; but like all political dogmatists he quarrelled bitterly and unforgivingly. Those who were cast into darkness did not return to the light. Also Péguy's preoccupation with Joan of Arc offended, even disgusted, many of his more politically-minded companions, who regarded religion as one of socialism's foremost enemies. As Péguy's own views moved closer to the Catholicism which he had rejected as a young man, his isolation intensified—even from his wife, who could not be told at first of his return to faith.

Péguy spent all his working life within sight of the Sorbonne, on which he had turned his back for the sake of a cause he thought more important. He believed that modern man suffered from a disease that attacked him within. The social revolution had to begin with the revolution of ourselves; the social and moral revolution were one and the same thing. He regarded the sickness of modern society as originating in three causes: the valuation of human labour in terms of economic profit, the failure of a metaphysic, and the triumph of science. 'It is probable,' he once wrote, 'that the most dangerous times in the life of a planet are those when science bankrupts hope. The ensuing fears are those which can destroy the spirit.' Péguy's hostility to the effects of science reflects what G. K. Chesterton described in the closing years of the nineteenth century as 'a curious cold air of emptiness and real subconscious agnosticism such as is extremely unusual in the history of mankind'. Péguy's analytical and rational methods of analysing the ills of the modern age quickly asserted themselves in *Les Cahiers de la Quinzaine*. Gradually, however, his determination to reform the values of society was modified by the recognition of the impossibility of the task without the operation of some form of grace. Unlike those more intransigently political than himself, his inner recognition of the reality of the spiritual life reached out and transformed the manner in which he expressed his political beliefs.

Péguy's preoccupation with Joan of Arc spans the whole of his life as a writer from 1893 to 1913. The repetition of theme is matched by a style peculiarly Péguy's own, in which the cadence of phrases, amplifying, reflecting and confirming each other, creates a musical effect that cannot be imitated successfully in translation. This mode of writing becomes more pronounced as Péguy's life progresses; but it is present even in his first *Joan of Arc* play (1897). It would be difficult to imagine a style apparently more undramatic, with its long deliberative speeches and phrases. They are sustained by an underlying rhythm expressing his sense of 'la souffrance humaine': itself the product of his determination never to give way before life, and his struggle to assert the values he believed it contained. The dramatic conflict itself arises from Joan's struggle to know what is right for her—as a means of bearing witness to the truth within her—rather than from the conflict between her and others. In the second *Joan of Arc* play (1910) the number of characters has been reduced to three, and the form of the chronicle play has almost entirely disappeared.

In his first dramatisation of the theme, Péguy openly admits in his dedication the close relationship for him between a political and a metaphysical cause: 'To all the men and women who will die trying to find a remedy for universal ill . . . for all those men and women who will die a human death for the creation of a universal socialist republic.'[3] As was to become increasingly clear in his later work, socialism embodied for him the mystery of charity. Joan at Domrémy is portrayed as suffering deeply from her awareness of the country being laid waste by the English. She suffers, she prays:

> O mon Dieu,
> Vous avez donc laissé recommencer cela.
> Vous avez donc laissé les bandes ravageuses
> Enflamber nos maisons, nos granges et nos blés;
> Et vous avez laissé les bandes outrageuses
> Enflamber la maison qui nous garde assemblés
> Pour la prière humaine et pour penser á vous.*[4]

But Joan has also to act for the purpose of trying to find a remedy for universal ill. And here she symbolises what all men and women must do in order to play their part in the creation of the harmonious city. In the event, actual action proves to involve a suffering different and worse to the suffering she had known in the isolation of Domrémy. She is

---

* O my God, you have thus allowed that to start again. You have thus allowed the ravaging troops to burn our homes, our farms and our crops, and you have allowed the scurrilous troops to burn the house which keeps watch over us, assembled for human prayer and for thinking of you.

horrified when Gilles de Rais tells her of the atrocities committed by the French in what she regards as a holy war:

> J'ai connu la souffrance, aussi, des trahisons.
> (*Un long silence.*)
> Mais je ne savais pas cette souffrance-là.
> Cette souffrance laide et sale et salissante.†[5]

Even so, commanded by God to leave Domrémy, she will not return to her father's house until her work has been done.

Péguy's drama is divided into three long plays—*Domrémy*, *Battles* and *Rouen* (each themselves subdivided into two or three sections, the length of an ordinary play). The slow enlargement and evolution of the action is amplified by the long silence, not only between the characters, but within the speeches themselves, as in the quotation above. This style is appropriate to the kind of drama at which Péguy is aiming, in which a constant self-questioning of motive and action is accompanied by an interrogation of Joan's claim to sainthood. The method of the play is profoundly analytic, and the analysis conjures up the conflict. The political scenes, which have disappeared in the later play, make less impact than those by Shaw and Anouilh on the same subject, since these scenes cannot be so centrally concerned with the intensity of Joan's struggle with herself, and what she should do. With his understanding of the French peasant Péguy can, however, represent more successfully than either of his successors the extraordinary leap that is involved in Joan's decision to leave Domrémy, and the huge act of faith involved in convincing the leaders of France of her mission. The agonised search through which Joan must go succeeds in becoming a particularised metaphor of all human suffering—and more especially that which arises out of a choice of action, or way of life. In her verse there accumulates the sound of a prolonged lament, both poignant and memorable:

> Mon âme est allée en la ville du siège,
> Avec les défenseurs qui s'acharnent là-bas.
> Mes pas vont s'éloigner tout à l'heure en la siège,
> Mais mon âme a passé dans le pays là-bas.
> (*Un silence*).
> Vous tous, que j'aimai tant quand j'étais avec vous
> O vous que j'aimai tant quand je m'en fus en France
> À présent, je vous aime encore plus, loin de vous:
> Mon âme a commencé l'étrange amour d'absence.*[6]

The grief serves also as a sign of deepening conviction.

In the second play, *Battles*, Joan has set out into the world, and though the play is concerned with her fight against the English, Joan has to struggle equally with her realisation of the atrocities committed by the Burgundians against their own countrymen, and to learn the meaning of defeat without despair. In the end even the King of France will reject her conviction that the English must be driven from France: 'Il est temps de vous reposer enfin; il faut vous reposer. Je le veux.'[7] Joan too must undergo initiation into the harshness of political realities that are wholly alien to her personality and faith. She hopes initially that the English may be persuaded, by the power of reason, to lay down their arms and leave France to its rightful inheritors. Even so, when she realises that force alone will drive them away, her weapon is a standard, not a sword. Killing revolts her. Joan's untarnished simplicity and directness (qualities which, as in Péguy's case, go with a certain lack of humour) make her convincing and real. The ecclesiastics whom she encounters are depicted as lacking these virtues. Péguy is concerned with that kind of integrity which exists among those who do not lose contact with the natural life of the earth on which they have grown up, and which nourishes in its most vital form their particular type of fortitude. Wealth and worldly power are inimical to it; their presence means not only a weakening of moral fibre, but a deviousness and willingness to compromise that Joan can never accept, and which she can only confront by an almost silent opposition.

The third part of the play, *Rouen*, is concerned with Joan's trial, and is the least successful. It lacks the intellectual thrust and openness of Shaw's political debates, which swiftly reveal the underlying intention behind political manoeuvring. As in *Battles*, Péguy's dramatic method succeeds best in moments of deliberation rather than physical action, in particular those that are concerned with Joan's struggle with herself. Knowing the meaning of defeat and rejection, facing the imminence

---

† I have known suffering, also betrayal. (*A long silence.*) But I did not know about suffering like this: suffering ugly and foul and fouling.

* My soul has gone out in the town of the siege, with the defenders who hold out down there; my steps are going to withdraw at once in the siege, but my soul has passed to the country down there. (*A silence.*) All you, whom I loved so much when I was with you, O you whom I loved so much when I was out of France, now I love you still more, being far away: my soul has begun the strange love of absence.

of death, she almost succumbs to the immensity of the struggle and the damnation of absence to which she feels herself condemned by her failure. Before going to be burnt, she is left only with the conviction that she has no course except to follow her voices, and that whatever harm she has done, the alternative to following them would have been worse. Through his austere and sombre view of things, Péguy makes us feel what is unbreakable in Joan, and we recognise this as the central human value in a world where everything else is dimmed by compromise and expedience. Joan confronts, accepts and acts upon reality— but, unlike Brand, without losing compassion for others who suffer in their own manner. As the historical trappings of the drama come to interest Péguy less, the values implicit in human action assume an increasingly central importance in his work.

Le Mystère de la Charité de Jeanne d'Arc (1910) reveals how far Péguy has withdrawn the boundaries of inner conflict. Once again a Catholic —but unable to accept the public face of Catholicism—the form of the chronicle play, and concern with characters more devious than Joan, have been pruned away. As the play progresses, Joan says less and less, leaving most of the talking to her spiritual adviser, Madame Gervaise. The only other character in the play is the ten-year-old Hauviette, whose conversation with Joan opens the action. The year is 1425. Joan, anxious, afraid for France, observes that after so many years of Christianity even the children go hungry still. Hauviette reproves her for thinking too much about the ills of yesterday and tomorrow, and suffering vicariously for others. But Joan can never accept the presence of evil. Her pity extends to a deep anxiety as to what she should do: prayer seems insufficient. She suffers for all that is happening in France, but she feels a sense of suffering beyond that, which she cannot explain; on this account she has come to see Madame Gervaise. Joan questions her as to whether she knows about the crimes of sacrilege the soldiers are committing in France; defiling the churches, drinking the sacramental wine, abusing the consecrated host. Their own opposition to all this exists only in the limited circle of their personal lives. She is filled with a sense of the absence of God.

Joan mediates on Christ's life, and on its significance for the lives of ordinary people; but when she comes to the abandonment of Christ by his disciples, she finds in herself a resistance. To Madame Gervaise's consternation, she asserts that if she had been there she does not think she would have abandoned him. Madame Gervaise warns her of the sin of pride; but Joan goes on to assert that neither the French knights nor the peasants would have abandoned him. The more she reiterates this, the more aware she becomes of the desolation around her. Madame Gervaise is taken aback by what she sees as an insult to the first saints of Christianity; but Joan can only repeat what she knows of the people of her own country: that they would not have betrayed and abandoned him. It is impossible that they would have committed the terrible crime of renunciation. Joan becomes increasingly preoccupied with the idea of not betraying the truth, and with the present movement of the Christian world towards perdition. Madame Gervaise warns her of human ignorance, of the inscrutability of God's ways and of the importance of prayer and faith. But the more Madame Gervaise says, the more Joan realises the impossibility for her of being content with a passive belief and a life of meditation. By the fall of the curtain she has turned towards Orléans, and the life of action through grace that it represents. It is this which constitutes her charity. To build the harmonious city, in whatever time and place one lives, it is necessary to act, and never to betray the faith that one has. Life means suffering; but through suffering too, charity is born.

The intense preoccupation of the play with the meaning of Christianity for Joan makes it a more private work than its predecessor. It speaks of the struggle which had brought Péguy back to Catholicism; and it celebrates the values which that faith involved for him. In *Le Porche du mystère de la deuxième vertu* (1911) his analysis of these values is taken one step further to include the one which ultimately mattered to him most. Madame Gervaise has become the sole speaker here; and in Péguy's verse—which more than ever turns upon itself, reiterates, moves relentlessly forward—she conveys how even more than love, the incredible and essential human possession is hope. It is easy, for her at least, to believe; and love, like faith, proceeds by itself. But hope springs from a mysterious concept of human life, that perfectibility is possible, human work not pointless, and life not arbitrary. The possibility of hope comes through Christ, and Grace. Much of the poem is once more taken up with meditation on the meaning of Christ's life. In its closing pages, however, it becomes a hymn for human hope. Hope brings renewal in the night of life; without it there would be only darkness and death. Through her vision Madame Gervaise becomes identified with God's own vision of his universe:

O nuit, ma plus belle invention, ma création auguste entre toutes.
Ma plus belle créature. Créature de la plus grande Espérance.
Qui donnes le plus de matière à l'Espérance.
Qui es l'instrument, qui es la matière même et la résidence de
l'Espérance.
Et aussi (et ainsi), au fond créature de la plus grande Charité.*[8]

It is not surprising that Péguy's sense of hope (a divine Hope,
'Espérance', not the human 'espoir') is born of the night. In spite of his
regained faith, his awareness of human suffering, and the spiritual
crisis which threatened the western world intensified as life went on.
To this was added his estrangement from his ardently socialist wife, as a
result of his newly found faith, and his deep but inhibited love for
another woman. In his later years too, the almost total lack of interest
shown in his poetry, and the failure of his *Cahiers* to retain their influence
as a forum for socialist ideas made his life an increasingly lonely
pilgrimage. This, however, did not shake—if anything it strengthened
—his belief in the possibility of human brotherhood, in the restoration
of dignity to human labour, and the possibility of combating the
falsely material values on which modern civilisation was based. About
1880, in his view, the modern age began; the old values were over-
turned, and the domination of people by the desire for material glory
began. Money became the standard of human judgement; and though
the bourgeoisie led the way in this respect, the whole responsibility did
not lie with them. The disease afflicted all parts of human society.
Péguy was not concerned with the class-struggle as such, nor with
economic theory. What mattered to him was the survival of Man's
spirit in an increasingly material world; and this, he believed, could not
be achieved by Man's agency alone. He disliked a great deal about the
Catholic Church; but he saw no prospect of a fairer human society
except through the operation of grace.

Of all the writers in this book Péguy is the most inward. His
chromatic style in the Joan plays projects the conflicts of the inner life:
the suffering of the individual in remaining true to what he sees as his
reality, and acting upon its demands. Much in the specifically Christian

---

* O night, my most beautiful invention, the noblest of my creations, my
most beautiful creature. Creature of the greatest Hope, who gives the most
substance to Hope. You are the instrument, the substance itself, and the abode of
Hope. And also, and thus, at root, the creature of the greatest Charity.

mediation of the works may not now have general appeal; much in them is repetitive, and too drawn-out. But Péguy's style at its best is taut, stringent, sharply directed: its music works to convey the depth and subtlety of his feeling. The long travail of his agonising originates in his perception of social injustice, and in his personal sense of in-adequacy before it. Life tormented Péguy ceaselessly; but he found in himself the difficulty and possibility of hope. He must stand in this book for that continuing tradition of writers who still saw in some form of Christianity the one real possibility of an art of celebration. In the literature of the twentieth century they have remained a positive and powerful force.

GEORGE BERNARD SHAW

... the theatre ... a factory of thought, a prompter of conscience, an
elucidator of social conduct, an armory against despair and dullness,
and a temple of the Ascent of Man. ...

G. B. Shaw: *Our Theatres in the Nineties* ... (1906)

In his 'Journal' for May 27, 1888, the young Bertrand Russell wrote:
We stand in want of a new Luther to renew faith and invigorate
Christianity and to do what the Unitarians would do if only they
had a really great man such as Luther to lead them. For religions grow
old like trees unless reformed from time to time. Christianity of the
existing kinds has had its day. We want a new form in accordance
with science and yet helpful to a good life.[1]
Shaw played the new Luther—with considerably more charm and wit.
Like Mr. Amarinth in *The Green Carnation*, he recognised that faith
was the most plural thing he knew; but the many churches of his time
(Burnes-Jonesian, Pasteurian, Marxist, Darwinian, Browningite) were
the property of the few; and the majority were simply becoming
heathen. This was a situation he did not relish, as he rightly saw that
neither individuals nor societies function well unless they have some
view of how things are, and how they should be. It was the role of the
philosopher-artist (the only kind of artist he took 'quite seriously') to
provide people with a usable doctrine. In one of his later plays, *Too
True to be Good* (1934), he expressed what had long since been his view
of society, and his relationship to it:
... We have outgrown our religion, outgrown our political system,
outgrown our own strength of mind and character ... all I know
is that I must find the way of life, for myself and all of us, or we shall
surely perish. ...[2]
Shaw once described himself as one of life's 'downstarts'. The son of
a declining middle-class family, he quickly grasped the importance of
money. But a highly developed aesthetic and musical personality,
inherited from his mother, also gave him an early distaste for 'Adam on
the make', and for the gross inequalities of nineteenth-century capitalist

society. Under the influence of Karl Marx he overcame the lack of any effective belief, and established himself as the leading practitioner of a deliberately propagandist theatre. Here Shaw's innate artistry, together with the experience gained as a dramatic critic, served him well. He knew that any good play, whatever its subject, must be local and its persons real as well as interesting. A conscience about slum-landlordism or prostitution would not in itself ensure success in the theatre; more probably it would simply mean censorship. After defeating the censor, Shaw also won his audience by his wit, and a schoolboy sense of fun—both of which he used to considerable dramatic effect. He enjoyed nothing more than seeing people slip on their own moral banana-peels; and he took advantage of this taste in the construction of his plays, where shifts of thought and situation reveal the moral humbug and pretence of respectability upon which society depends in order to continue to think well of itself. Like their creator, in terms of initial economic disadvantage, Shaw's characters were also swimmers, not sinkers. In a crooked society, he enjoyed displaying how the most talented and imaginative crooks were able to turn the tables to their own advantage. But this love of buoyancy did not obscure, from him or his audience, how high the price of victory could be, nor how squalid were the conditions which made victory essential.

Mrs. Warren's Profession (1894) is among the best of Shaw's early plays, and among the most vilified at the time. In an agreeable Surrey garden, the practical, self-reliant and ambitious young Vivie Warren awaits the arrival of her mother, whom she scarcely knows. Vivie has received a university education, and personifies the virtues of a secure middle-class upbringing. Her mother has not enjoyed her privileges. She reveals to her daughter that in her youth she chose to become a prostitute rather than face an early death from penury, forced labour and undernourishment. Vivie can sympathise with her choice until she learns from Sir George Crofts, her mother's business partner, that their money is still derived from high-class brothels in Europe. Vivie leaves home at once, sets up in business, and refuses not only her mother's money, but her affection and friendship. She explains:

> Yes: it's better to choose your line and go through with it. If I had been you, mother, I might have done as you did; but I should not have lived one life and believed in another. You are a conventional woman at heart. That is why I am bidding you good-bye now.[3]

Shaw shows no lack of sympathy for Mrs. Warren's initiative, skill and good business-sense; but her desire to appear respectable while living off the money derived from vice appals him no less than the social conditions which once turned her into a prostitute. Shaw sees corruption everywhere: even Vivie's scholarship at Newnham has been established by an M.P. who gets twenty-two per cent out of a factory with six hundred girls in it, and not one of them getting enough wages to live on. The final scene of the play turns upon Vivie's rejection of her mother. Mrs. Warren is hurt and angered by her daughter's desire not to see her again; and Shaw has portrayed her, in her robust vulgarity, as decidedly likeable. But Vivie's mood, once the link has been broken, is one of joyous content. Liberation from her mother, and from her feckless lover, means she can get down to the serious business of earning her living as an actuary. Vivie's need for liberation might seem to resemble Nora's in *A Doll's House*; but in spite of Shaw's admiration for Ibsen, their plays—both in structure and effect —have little in common.

What Mrs. Warren reveals about her past is not intended only to advance the action, but to inform the audience of its moral blindness and responsibility for social injustice. Shaw used dramatic reversal to startle his audience into new awareness about themselves, or their assumptions. His views were not flattering; but because his plays often depended upon a 'wicked' person who turned out to be more right than those who believed themselves good, he never sounded high-mindedly moralistic. The intelligence which enabled such a person to detect what the world was really like, and use this realism for his (or her) advantage, aroused his sympathy for their courage and conviction. Only his less competent 'villains'—for example, Sir George Crofts in *Mrs. Warren's Profession*—display the meanness and nastiness which frequently accompanies cynicism. In a situation of moral corruption, such as Shaw perceived around him, the benevolent despot and moral realist stood far more chance of improving the fortunes of others than those who went about doing good, or doing ill half-heartedly. For all his social concern, Shaw was most interested by people of exceptional energy, imagination and will, whether this turned them into saints or millionaires.

In two very different plays of the pre-war period, *Caesar and Cleopatra* (1898) and *Major Barbara* (1907), Shaw made his central character a man of unusual ability. In the prologue to *Caesar and Cleopatra* (not written in its final form until 1912) Caesar addressed his audience of self-deceived imperialists directly. Through the voice of the great god Ra, he warned them of the real nature of their Empire. Based like all other empires before it on boasting, injustice, lust and stupidity, it too would one day be swept away. The play itself—though it included much buffoonery which was far from Shaw at his best—portrayed a Caesar who was great because he had no illusions about the nature of his power, or the manner in which it had been acquired: 'The road to riches and greatness', he admits, 'is through robbery of the poor and slaughter of the weak.'[4] Our so-called morality is based on the same foundation. To the end of history murder will breed murder, 'always in the name of honour and right and peace, until the gods are tired of blood and create a race that can understand'.[5] So far the human race has not progressed in this direction: 'All the savagery, barbarism, dark ages and the rest of it of which we have any record as existing in the past exists in the present moment.'[6] Caesar's outstanding ability, which has made him master of the Roman Empire, had not blinded him to the barbarism which Empire involves; he knows that in the end his power depends on the means and willingness to kill.

But while Caesar remains decisive in action, his more reflective moments show little relish for his role. When Cleopatra admits to the murder of Pothinus, Caesar comments: 'If one man in all the world can be found, now or forever, to know that you did wrong, that man will either have to conquer the world, as I have, or be crucified by it.'[7] Caesar's awareness of what he is, and what he has done, is pointedly contrasted with Cleopatra's wayward and ruthless enjoyment of her own power, and Rufio's blunt commitment to being an effective soldier. In spite of the portrayal of Caesar's greatness as the product of his realism and humanity, the play does not wholly succeed, because the minor characters lack sufficient depth for the theme; and Shaw persistently trivialises it by failing to sustain an appropriate imaginative level: the inclusion of Britannus, for example, to provide an opportunity for jokes about the English serves no useful dramatic end.

Major Barbara is a more closely worked and deeply apprehended work. Andrew Undershaft has long since been rejected by his wife as an extremely immoral man. His children, while being brought up on the money derived from his fabulously successful iron foundry, have not been permitted to meet him; but the prospect of their marriages and careers has compelled his wife to admit her inability to cope without his assistance. As Lady Britomart warns her son, Stephen, Andrew Undershaft's wickedness takes unusual forms. He plans to follow the Undershaft tradition and disinherit Stephen for a foundling, who will run the foundry. Shaw's play is based on a simple and essentially comic device: the confrontation between members of a family who have long since become strangers. Its particular originality arises from the conflict between Barbara Undershaft, a dedicated Salvation Army worker, and her father, upon whose money she finds herself depending for the continuation of her good work. Undershaft believes that poverty is a crime. An East-Ender who started with nothing, he swore that the next man should starve before he did. His determination and energy have enabled him to create a fortune out of his munitions factory, and to build, as his family discover to their chagrin in the final act, an earthly city as close to a heavenly one as it can be: it includes nursing-homes, libraries, schools and every sign of a proper civic spirit. In Undershaft's experience, money and gunpowder are essential before you can afford the luxuries of honour, love, justice, truth and so forth. Freed from poverty, he has become useful, beneficent and kindly: 'That is the history of most self-made millionaires, I fancy. When it is the history of every Englishman we shall have an England worth living in.'[8]

In Undershaft Shaw once more creates a man of imagination and realism; his likeableness and generosity are paradoxically contrasted with the death and destruction in which he deals. He is allowed too to evade a number of the issues which his conduct implicitly raises—for instance, another country's weapons never threaten his own model factory—but like Caesar he illustrates a central Shavian viewpoint: the skills of the most highly motivated, energetic and useful members of a community will reflect the moral climate in which they have to operate, since, by their very nature, they must work with things as they are, not with things as they ought to be. Shaw has no patience with the man who knows the difference between right and wrong, as Stephen does, but who has never tried himself in the actual world. Undershaft recognises that in the world as it exists the ultimate test of conviction is the willingness to kill; and the challenge with which he confronts his family is: if you don't like my 'religion', change the world so that it no longer applies. Or as he puts it to Cusins: 'Turn your oughts into shalls man. Come and make explosives with me. Whatever can blow men up can blow society up.'[9]

In Act Two, Undershaft visits the Salvation Army shelter in West Ham, threatened with closure by lack of funds. Bodger, 'the whisky king', has offered five thousand pounds if somebody else can be found to match it. Undershaft writes the cheque with playful disinterestedness: 'Well, it is your work to preach peace on earth and good will to men. Every convert you make is a vote against war. Yet I give you this money to help you hasten my own commercial ruin.'[10] Ironically, his generosity comes much closer to ruining his daughter. Unable to bear seeing the shelters kept open by drunkenness and murder, she resigns from the army and pins the badge on her father: 'There! It's not much for £5,000, is it?'[11] The irony and poignance of the moment is memorable. But both Undershaft and Barbara recover, because Shaw attributes to them, and admires in them, the resilience to do so.

In spite of his moral realism, Shaw did not become a cynic. The Undershaft Factory and Community at Perivale Saint Andrews is meant to represent a real view of what a clean, well-organised and efficient industrial township could be like. Shaw believed in people being well fed, clothed, housed and educated; and he saw no reason why this should not come about, if they were taught to demand it. Undershaft's doctrine that killing is the final test of conviction is also challenged by Cusins, the teacher of Greek, whom Undershaft adopts as the foundling: 'It is historically true. I loathe having to admit it. I repudiate your sentiments. I abhor your nature. I defy you in every possible way. Still it is true. But it ought not to be true.'[12] Cusins joins Undershaft with a purpose: 'As a teacher of Greek I gave the intellectual man weapons against the common man. I now want to give the common man weapons against the intellectual man . . . I want a power simple enough to force . . . the intellectual oligarchy to use its genius for the common good.'[13] Cusins is not at all clear what this power will be, except that he intends to make war on war. Barbara, to whom he is engaged, expresses the vision poetically: 'the raising of hell to Heaven, and of man to God. . . .'[14] Both recognise that the only chance of putting an end to the Undershaft religion lies in changing man's moral nature so that all men work for the common good.

The play is sustained by powerful convictions, tempered by comic inventiveness. Dolly and her incorrigibly empty-headed suitor are incapable of taking things seriously, while Stephen is much too earnest to be taken seriously by anyone else. The setting of Act Two in the West Ham shelter lay well outside Shaw's dramatic range, since he could not conceive of dialogue except as a statement and riposte; and his ability to create either irrational or 'inarticulate' characters was severely limited. However it serves to suggest, at least embryonically, the violence which Undershaft appears to have mastered. But it leaves no shadow upon an ending where happiness is possible because everyone behaves with intelligence and restraint, and the assured world they inhabit suffers no external threat.

Major Barbara—implicitly at least—celebrates the existence of such qualities in human life, without obscuring the violent amorality with which human affairs are ultimately conducted. In earlier plays Shaw had persistently questioned contemporary attitudes, and their underlying assumptions. In *Arms and the Man* he exposed the inadequacy of the popular view of romantic love: that the partners were necessarily faithful; and of war: that the victors were really heroic. *The Devil's Disciple* portrayed a social outcast and rebel of much greater humanity than those who spurned him; and a priest who served his fellow men better in action than in the pulpit. And *Candida* dealt with a choice in marriage made pragmatically and rightly in terms of need. Shaw regarded the majority of emotional and social attitudes of his time as shallow. He possessed an extensive moral distaste for the manner in which human beings conducted their affairs; but this did not lead, as with Swift, to a savage indignation. His exuberance was used to expose human delusion in a wide variety of dramatic forms, and with ample theatrical skill. But, as in the cartoon film, behaviour, however bad, seldom led to real harm.

Shaw's high spirits in the theatre were perhaps a means of self-protection, since he certainly believed that if Man was going to survive he had to find some way of turning himself into a better and more efficient being. Socialism was an indispensable step in the right direction —but no more than a step, since Man would always return to his idols and cupidities, in spite of all revolutions and movements, until his nature was changed. The only hope lay in the evolution of some higher form of being. Here Shaw the philosopher took over from Shaw the artist.

Shaw first stated his evolutionary philosophy in Act Three of *Man and Superman* (1903); twenty years later he elaborated upon it in the 'Preface' to *Back to Methuselah* (1921). By then the First World War had done much to confirm his fears as to whether—in spite of the promise of socialism—the human animal was capable of solving the problems raised by his civilisation. At any rate it could not be done without a religion of some sort. The only one which he perceived to have a 'scientific basis' was that of Creative Evolution—itself a reaction against what seemed to him the mechanistic and haphazard theory of evolution proposed by Darwin. Shaw believed this to be dangerous and untrue because it left to chance (natural selection) what he believed was a matter of will. He therefore became the champion of the older view of evolution, proposed by Lamarck, in which development occurred through the application of will and the inheritance of acquired character-istics. If Man was to be saved, he must save himself. Jack Tanner—alias Don Juan—became the mouthpiece of his doctrine in *Man and Superman*:

> I tell you that as long as I can conceive something better than myself I cannot be easy unless I am striving to bring it into existence or clearing the way for it. That is the law of my life. That is the working within me of Life's incessant aspiration to higher organisa-tion, wider, deeper, intenser, self-consciousness, and clearer self-understanding. It was the supremacy of this purpose that reduced love for me to the mere pleasure of a moment, art for me to the mere schooling of my faculties, religion for me to a mere excuse for laziness since it had set up a God who looked at the world, and saw that it was good, against the instinct in me that looked through my eyes at the world and saw that it could be improved.[15]

Tanner represents the will to be heroic in the face of weakness, and never to accept the way things are. The really damned are those who are happy in Hell—a place where you do nothing but amuse yourself. Heaven is abrasive, challenging and austere. 'In Heaven you live and work'; and what you are working for is that higher understanding and intelligence which enables you to steer, not to drift, 'to be able to choose the line of greatest advantage instead of yielding in the direction of the least resistance'.[16] Only such a change in Man's nature would put an end to the cycle in which revolutions merely 'shifted the burden of tyranny from one shoulder to another'.

The dream sequence in Act Three of *Man and Superman* contains the greater part of the play's philosophic discussion. Shaw sustains it with his usual verve and conviction; but it occurs within a play of unusually little intellectual interest. Shaw's intention of writing a Don Juan play—with the woman as huntress—thinly disguises an equally old theme: that of the bachelor reluctant to wed. The surrounding action is also contrived from a play of types, not persons—with Henry Straker as the knowing servant, Roebuck Ramsden as the older man outraged by the morals of the young, and Hector Malone as the father disposed to disinherit his daughter if she marries without his consent. The play is saved by the inexhaustible verbal dash and audacity of Jack Tanner, who uses his exceptionally sharp wits to cause consternation at every opportunity, without finally evading the trap being set for him by Ann. The unity of the play depends upon a contrast between an elegant comedy about conventional attitudes towards love, women and family relationships; and Tanner's proposals for the 'Ascent of Man', propounded in Act Three. In each, Shaw deluges his audience with words —words that cause delight by their unexpectedness, and their revelations of quick turns of thought. The acrobatics are unflaggingly sustained; but the language does not penetrate deeply. A swordsman as deft as Shaw can make palpable hits (and he does); but the showmanship of the feint or parry distracts attention from the seriousness of the fight. The play is an elegant and original piece of theatre; but its ideas do not disturb.

Back to Methuselah attempts to dramatise Shaw's philosophy of creative evolution at work. By the end of the play we are to believe ourselves carried as far forward as thought can reach—some thirty thousand years in this case. Inevitably the subject matter remains speculative. But if the detail remains of increasingly insubstantial dramatic interest, the play is sustained by a vision of undeniable importance. When Lilith at the close reviews man's progress, his victory over ageing and the lusts of the flesh, she still sees the chief human virtue as not being satisfied:

> ... After passing a million goals they press on to the goal of redemption from the flesh, to the vortex freed from matter, to the whirlpool in pure intelligence that, when the world began, was a whirlpool in pure force.[17]

Shaw's vision of the ascent of Man through willed development of higher intelligence contains a great deal of emotional appeal which, in spite of the extended dramatic development, is by no means entirely lost.

Shaw always poses the problem of how seriously he should be taken, or even intended to be. Undoubtedly, he enjoyed nothing more than wittily exposing the inadequacies of contemporary assumptions, and the outrageousness of contemporary behaviour. For an Irishman living

F

in England, the time for practising the art of upsetting the apple-cart was propitious. England at the zenith of its commercial and imperial power was a fair enough target; and Shaw shared with England the conviction of being right. He enjoyed warning the English that the wealth and the glory were only a matchwood bridge over the abyss; and the English enjoyed having this pointed out to them, because the bridge still held. The debate could be conducted in a civilised, even light-hearted, manner. But no one can read far in Shaw without realising that he shared with a good many men before and since a horror at the manner in which human beings organised their lives and their communities. One can therefore scarcely quarrel with Shaw for seeing the urgency of finding a new philosophy, nor can one relegate that to some minor position in his view of things as an artist. As Sempronius says in *The Apple Cart* (1929): 'Who could be dull with pools in the rocks to watch? Yet my father, with all that under his nose, was driven mad by its nothingness.'[18] Nor can one quarrel with Shaw's contention that Man in his present form is scarcely likely to overcome the flaws in him which make his idols and cupidities so potent and destructive. Shaw believed that he saw a way through; and it would be to slight the importance he attached to the artist-philosopher to give that solution anything less than a central importance. Shaw without the 'why not' (which could not be defined in merely political terms) would not be Shaw. And Shaw intended to be something more than a *farceur*.

The difficulty of taking Shaw seriously originates not only in the solution, but in the formulation of the problem. In Shaw's world, everyone thinks and behaves in a Shavian manner: they are capable of resolving their differences because they can argue rationally about them. Unwillingness to listen and inability to articulate have no place in his landscape. At the end of both *Man and Superman* and *Too True to be Good*, the central character is left only with the power of words. Even if a Shavian character does nothing constructive, he can at least go on talking, and talking very well. At least on the surface, such a world is witty and rational; but the things of which Shaw's characters often talk suggest a reality of a very different kind. Shaw—alias Jack Tanner —thought all men should be 'masters of reality'; but it is arguable whether he himself was. He saw where many serious and intolerable problems existed; but his manner of solving them remained part of the graceful world he constructed to illustrate them.

In two plays not yet mentioned, *Heartbreak House* (1919) and *Saint Joan* (1924), the façade of civilised conversation admits—at least glancingly—the presence of forces that may not be easily controlled. In the earlier play, Captain Shotover is symbolic of a society that has lost its sense of direction and purpose. Like some of Shaw's previous heroes, he prefers hardship to ease, and is happier on a bridge in a typhoon than in any pursuit of pleasure or love. Yet in his old age he is concerned only with an almost dotty desire to achieve the seventh degree of concentration. Meanwhile the ship of which he is his master lacks any helmsman. He is surrounded by people as amusing and useless as they can be. Some, at least, know how futile their way of life has become; and that the bomb which falls at the bottom of the garden presages doom upon it. But knowledge of disaster ahead does not make them alter their course, or even show any desire to do anything about it. They continue to live, as they always have, in their circumscribed world of light loves and passing commitments. In *Saint Joan*, Shaw conceives a character willing to make the necessary sacrifice for the purpose of restoring order and decency in human society; but she is inevitably opposed by those who feel their own power threatened; and this means not only the threat to the authority of individuals, but to the institutionalised power of the State, the Church and the Monarchy. Joan has to die, because they cannot afford to allow her to challenge their interests, or the rightness of their disposal of human affairs. Joan's real crime, as the English chaplain points out, is that she is a rebel; and her vision of truth conflicts irreconcilably with the values by which others live. Like Christ in *The Brothers Karamazov*, Joan would need to be killed again if she reappeared in a later age, since the time for the saints has not yet come.

Saint Joan is the one play in which Shaw's vision approaches the tragic; and it is written with a depth of feeling that gives Joan the power to move, as Shaw's characters rarely do. But Shaw's major contribution to the theatre did not lie in extending our awareness of the insoluble and arbitrary problems of the human condition. He used the theatre to argue incessantly for a more rational organisation of human affairs; and in doing so, he inevitably called into question the correctness and relativity of his viewpoint. Like his own character, Caesar, Shaw had the virtue of infinite courage: 'He who has never hoped can never despair. Caesar, in good or bad fortune, looks his fate in the face.'[19] While his philosophy of creative evolution may appeal to few as a substitute for religion, it expresses a part of a common human hope; that, in however gradual a way, the sum of human good may increase to the point at which destructive individual passions are mastered, and social evils overcome. Shaw with his sane lack of an overwrought emotional involvement (now very rare) makes us see, and makes us laugh. As a literary artist he does not rank with Hardy or Conrad; as a dramatist with Ibsen or Chekov. But what he lacks in depth, he compensates for in exuberance, intelligence, and zest. His energy and his wit gave him an inexhaustible talent for enjoying himself; and he communicates that enjoyment in spite of the sombreness of his themes. Without ever being morbid, Shaw believed there was no purpose in living unless you were determined to leave things better than you found them. His art is committed to that end; and its hope, which finds expression in all that he wrote, makes possible the celebration of life.

11

H. G. WELLS

If one does not accept the general ideas upon which the existing world of man is based, one is bound to set about replanning and reconstructing the world on the ideas one finds acceptable.

H. G. Wells: *Experiment in Autobiography* (1934)

Wells shared with Shaw a dislike for the Yellow Nineties, and its taste for aestheticism. Both men regarded themselves as realistic and anti-romantic. But in temperament, and as writers, the two men were very different. Wells put it like this in his *Autobiography*:

We were both atheists and socialists; we were both attacking an apparently fixed and invincible social system from the outside; but this much resemblance did not prevent our carrying ourselves with a certain defensiveness towards each other that remains to this day. . . . (Shaw) thinks one can 'put things over' on Fact and I do not.[1]

The comment reveals characteristic English mistrust of the Irish; but it brings out an important difference between the two men as writers. Shaw, for all his range of knowledge and allusion (notably in the 'Prefaces') and in spite of his prejudice, was a more aesthetic writer than Wells. Wells had variousness, energy and inventiveness; but Shaw —if one considers only the profusion of dramatic modes in which he worked—was a more conscious and deliberate artist.

The form of Wells's novels and stories was controlled by the ideas he wished to explore; and they are always closely related to his own wide-ranging speculations upon the meaning of human history, and upon the possibilities for a future, shaped by social and scientific change. He had no great talent for the creation of fictional characters; and even his most celebrated—Kipps and Mr. Polly—are imprinted with aspects of his own autobiography. As with all writers of ideas, some at least of his interests derive from the immediate preoccupations of his time. But his inventiveness in exploring the probable effects of man's new tech-nological and scientific knowledge (and his warnings of the dangers inherent in their abuse) created a form of fiction in which fantasy and truth were skilfully balanced. The shrewdness of Wells's judgement

F*

about the shape of things to come, and the changes already at work in society, enabled him to remain within the bounds of the possible.

At the age of eleven or twelve, Wells tells us, 'religion began to fall to pieces in his consciousness.'[2] In time this led him to ask the questions which inevitably occur to an inquiring mind: 'In the absence of God what was this universe, and how was it run?'[3] As for most people, the second question proved easier to answer than the first. Wells, like Shaw, saw it as run wastefully, destructively, and with potentially catastrophic results for the survival of the human race. A great deal of his life was spent in thinking, arguing and agitating for changes which would reduce the incidence of waste, and the possibility of calamity. The goal of men who thought about the predicament of Man in the twentieth century must be 'to rescue human society from the net of tradition in which it is entangled and to reconstruct it upon planetary lines'.[4] Wells's philosophy grew and crystallised in the later part of his life; its origins lay in his works of fiction, both scientific and social, and his essays and prophecies, which were turned out in profusion. In them a blunt, honest common sense distinguishes him at once, as he rightly saw, from the more fanciful Shaw. But the temper of his mind turns out to be no less idealistic.

Wells's preoccupation with the future, apparent in his fiction, owes a great deal to the influence upon him of evolutionary theory, which he assimilated at the Royal College of Science, where he was taught for a time by T. H. Huxley. At this time too he came to recognise the enormous and new importance of science in the development of human thought and civilisation. Any new formulation of how the world might be changed for the better would now take into account the new perspectives it had created: 'The Utopia of a modern dreamer must needs differ in one fundamental aspect from the Nowheres and Utopias men planned before Darwin quickened the thought of the world.'[5] Man was the product of a struggle for existence which made him incurably egoistic and aggressive; he lived on a planet on which nothing endured, and where all was subject to fluctuation and change. The dilemma for him was what he made out of these unpromising conditions, and how he could achieve a state in which the struggle for power and jealousy no longer dominated the organisation of national and international communities.

Wells's early fiction may be divided into two broad categories: the social novels, which are centrally concerned with the waste of life in the present organisation of society; and the scientific fantasies, which concentrate for the most part on the potentially disastrous consequences of Man's abusing his new understanding of the material universe. His attitudes, if not his artistic formulation of them, have much in common with those of Shaw in the first; but in the second his scientific knowledge resulted in a more pessimistic emphasis.

In his visions of the future Wells manipulates a knowledge of carefully selected scientific facts to give plausibility to his tale; but he is also working upon fears and doubts that relate to his own time, and which the tale of the future serves to amplify and illuminate. *The Time Machine* (1895) is a tale of this sort. It opens at a gathering of scientific persons, not much inclined to credit what they are being told, and representative of a group to which Wells could be sure a large number of his readers would like to belong:

> The time traveller (for so it will be convenient to speak of him) was expounding a recondite matter to us. His grey eyes shone and twinkled, and his usually pale face was flushed and animated. The fire burned brightly, and the soft radiance of the incandescent lights in the lilies of silver caught the bubbles that flashed and passed in our glasses.[6]

But the time traveller has more than a theory to offer; he has created the model of a machine capable, as he believes, of carrying him backwards and forwards in time, as easily as a carriage normally carries people in space.

The main part of the subsequent narrative is concerned with his account of a journey into the future. What he discovers by landing some six thousand years hence is conceived as a frightening adventure; but its point is to expose the possible result of man's continuing to live by his present values. He encounters a society of small, pink-faced people who appear to live without hardship or distress. Scientific progress has long since overcome the struggle for existence; and the Eloi, as they are called, have succumbed to the feebleness which results from the cessation of need. The human intellect has committed suicide; and the impulse to create art has turned into languor and decay. But the intellectual decline of the Eloi represents only half the darkness which the time traveller discovers; society is still divided into the Haves and Have-nots. Beneath the surface of the earth live the Morlocks, the descendants of the labourers who had worked to ensure the pleasures and comforts of the capitalists; now, though, they emerge from their subterranean world at night to feed on the enfeebled bodies of the Eloi, who have lost the will to resist. The time traveller himself only escapes by a hair's-breadth from their trap for him, by once again propelling himself through time.

The two species which Wells envisages as resulting from contemporary society are both in their own way equally depressing and unpleasant: Wells projects upon them his own distaste for the pampered indolence of the upper bourgeoisie, and his equally intense dislike of the slave mentality to which, if he had not possessed so much energy and talent, he might have succumbed. Further on in time, the traveller discovers a world desolate of human life, and inhabited by monstrous crabs. Both this desolation and the previous terror of his encounter with the Morlocks cast their shadows back upon the present, and the direction in which its combination of knowledge and inequalities might lead. Wells skilfully enforces the point by describing the landscape of the future as visually unchanged. The time traveller still walks beside the Thames; but the signs of a purposeful and civilised society have either disappeared or stand in ruins. The society of the future becomes an exaggerated metaphor for the worst aspects of the present, and a warning of the need for change.

The Time Machine is focused upon the condition of society; *The Island of Doctor Moreau* (1896) and *The Invisible Man* (1897) upon the precarious stability of the individual. In each, he depicts the power which science has given to Man without making him correspondingly stronger in the ability to control his passions, or in his fundamental humanity. In *The Island of Doctor Moreau*, the scientist is portrayed as a man who, not believing in God, takes on himself God's role as maker. Uncontrolled by any moral code, or any awareness of his own limitations, he attempts to create a new kind of man out of animals. To Prendick, the unfortunate observer of his grotesque experiment he explains: 'The study of Nature makes a man at last as remorseless as Nature. . . .'[7] Dr. Moreau exemplifies the abuse of scientific knowledge, through ignorance of what science can presently achieve, and through the false pride which it encourages in those who possess it. Wells was more variously aware than any other writer of his time of the changes that were shortly to occur through advances in scientific knowledge. He understood the implications of increasingly sophisticated weapons for subduing or exterminating human life—both in the context of a mechanised urban society, and of warfare. He foresaw the importance of domination in the air, and possibility of an atom bomb. And he recognised the inadequacy of the individual as a custodian for these new powers. Dr. Moreau himself is conceived as a 'theological grotesque', willing to inflict appalling pain on the animals in his island for the purpose of turning them into his slaves. But the law which he attempts to impose upon them through vivisection proves incapable of controlling instincts and behavioural patterns, developed over long periods of time.

Dr. Moreau personifies that impatience and crudeness of method which comes from failing to understand the moral challenge of new knowledge, and the limitations of what it makes possible. Moreau not only wants to play God, but also to modify the evolutionary process without understanding how it works. But the 'nightmare' of what occurs on the island has its parallel in the ordinary human world. When Prendick, the observer of Moreau's experiments, escapes from the island, he sees his fellow human beings differently: '. . . I go in fear. I see faces keen and bright, others dull or dangerous, others unsteady, insincere; none that have the calm authority of a reasonable soul. . . .'[8] The people of London appear to him no better than another kind of beast-people. He feels this to be a disease he has brought back with him from the island, which can only be assuaged by the stillness of Nature; but it reflects the tale's central point: the primitiveness of man in spite of his apparent knowledge, and the ease with which he can revert to bestial forms of behaviour.

In *The Invisible Man*, Griffin, 'the most gifted physicist the world has ever known', learns how to make it impossible for others to see him. His strange and terrible career ends in disaster because he chooses to abuse the power which his discovery gives him. Wells initiates his tale of mystery and fear with an old device: the arrival of a muffled stranger in a country inn. The development of tension is intensified by the normality of life against which the stranger's peculiar activities and behaviour are seen. Wells's brisk manner is well suited to the depiction of the bustle and gossip of everyday life; and unaffected though such life is by important ideas and events, it reveals the humanity which Griffin's life lacks. He is willing to rob his father when he needs money for his research; and although this crime leads to his father's suicide, he suffers no remorse. As with Moreau, the claims of science overrule those of morality; and the discovery of how to become invisible serves only to intensify his fantasies of power.

Wells conceives the tale as a series of encounters between the villagers and Griffin, who grows increasingly aggressive and violent as the advantages of his new situation occur to him; and Wells directly involves the reader by compelling him to imagine the situation:

> You must figure the street full of running figures, of doors slamming, and fights for hiding-places. You must figure the tumult suddenly striking on the unstable equilibrium of old Fletcher's planks and two chairs—with cataclysmal results ... Everywhere there is a sound of closing shutters and shoving bolts, and the only visible humanity is an occasional flitting eye under a raised eyebrow in the corner of a window-pane.[9]

The method is not sophisticated; but it is effective: not only in conveying the fear which Griffin's violence arouses, but also in making apparent how his abuse of power isolates him from others. When he is compelled to seek a confederate and helper, he also reveals the extent of his inner corruption: he is indifferent to the suffering he has caused, and he intends to usher in the new epoch of the invisible man with a reign of terror. When he dies, his physical form reappears, imprinted with the horror of his experience:

> ... there lay, naked and pitiful on the ground, the bruised and broken body of a young man about thirty. ... His hands were clenched, his eyes wide open and his expression was one of anger and dismay....[10]

Here, as in *The Island of Doctor Moreau*, Wells shows a deep scepticism about man's fitness for the extensions of power which science is putting in his hands. His depiction of the ordinary surface of life in an English village serves both as a contrast to the scientific fantasy, and as a means of illustrating the precariousness of order and organisation in the face of new and unexpected challenges.

The landing of the Martians in *The War of the Worlds* results in a disorientation on a far larger scale than in *The Invisible Man*; but both are concerned with the restricted experiences with which man is equipped to deal. The invasions of the Martians quickly undermines the human sense of natural superiority over other forms of life:

> I felt the first inkling of a thing that presently grew quite clear in my mind, that oppressed me for many days, a sense of dethronement, a persuasion that I was no longer master, but an animal among animals, under the Martian heel. With us it would be as with them, to lurk and watch, to run and hide; the fear and empire of man has passed away.[11]

The Martians succumb to disease; but their brief supremacy leaves an abiding sense of doubt and insecurity in the narrator's mind, and a changed view of the future:

> It has robbed us of that serene confidence in the future which is the most fruitful source of decadence, the gifts to human science it has brought are enormous, and it has done much to promote the conception of the commonweal of mankind.[12]

The idea of how human life might be improved on a planetary basis was never far from Wells's thought; and it arose out of his constant awareness of the muddle and waste and lack of planning in world organisation, which could easily lead to disaster. In *The Sleeper Awakes* he imagined the Europe of two hundred years hence; and he depicted the scientific utopia which had once been dreamed of as remote as ever. The crowd is a crowd still, helpless in the hands of demagogue and organiser, 'individually cowardly, individually swayed by appetite, collectively incalculable'. The growth of the city has been accompanied by the growth of poverty and helpless labour; it has become a great machine, dominated by the dogma and propaganda of Ostrog, who sees the mass of common men as a helpless unit, to be bullied and educated into the submission of a lifetime's drudgery. The inventions of science help to sustain the supremacy of the few over the many; and when resistance threatens to bring about ruthless suppression, the dream of the future ends in the fury of war.

Wells's fantasies about the future reflect his misgivings about the present, which are centrally portrayed in his social fiction. The heroes of *Kipps* (1905), *Tono-Bungay* (1909) and *The History of Mr. Polly* (1910) are threatened at the outset of their lives with the drudgery which the social system of late nineteenth-century England imposes upon its less fortunate sons, unless they, like Wells, succeed in breaking out of their bondage. We first meet Mr. Polly, one of Wells's most endearing creations, sitting on a stile, aged thirty-seven and a half, proclaiming that the town of Fishbourne where he lives is a 'beastly silly wheeze of a hole!' His attitude is partly the result of the indigestion brought on by his wife's unhealthy cooking; but Mr. Polly has also come to find the whole of his life excessive and inadequate. Doomed to being a small town shopkeeper, kept company by a wife for whom he feels no sympathy, he still feels for life—outside the regions devastated by the school curriculum—an intense and frustrated curiosity. During his fifteen years of married misery in Fishbourne, the fire of his life has only been kept alive by his insatiable hunger for bright and delightful experience, for the gracious aspects of things, for beauty—and by his reading: 'Books that told of glorious places abroad and glorious times, that wrung a rich humour from life, and contained the delight of words freshly and expressively grouped'.[13] Mr. Polly is deprived at Fishbourne of the company of almost anyone to whom he can talk about what he enjoys; and his fate, as Wells sees it, 'netted in greyness and discomfort—with life dancing all about him' is that to which millions are condemned, while 'we lack "that collective will and intelligence" which would dam the streak of human failure.'[14]

Fortunately, for Mr. Polly, he shares Wells's view that if the world does not please you, you can change it—with a little bit of luck. Attempting suicide, he succeeds in setting light to his hateful shop, and on the proceeds of the insurance feels justified in leaving his wife (reserving twenty-one pounds for his immediate needs) and taking to the open road, which leads to the Potwell Inn. The world isn't Fishbourne, and the Potwell Inn, in spite of villainous Uncle Jim, is a good deal better. When we leave Mr. Polly, he is enjoying the beauty of a summer's evening, lost in the 'smooth, still quiet of the mind'. Wells's own life bore witness to the philosophy of Mr. Polly that 'there is only one sort of man who is absolutely to blame for his own misery, and that is the man who finds life dull and dreary.'[15] But this staunch individualism did not blind him to the social doom which can fall upon people, and which Mr. Polly so narrowly escapes.

Kipps too is well set for a lifetime as a draper's assistant, lost in an abyss of boredom, and conscious of a desire to get away from an environment in which he feels himself to be trapped. The apparent bounty of the gods in bequeathing him a fortune leads, on the other hand, to an increasing sense of isolation and futility. Intent upon building a more pretentious house than he needs (Wells is always militantly opposed to the material encumbrance of property) Kipps finds himself when the majority of his wealth disappears, 'standing among his foundations like a lonely figure among ruins.' The snobberies and pettiness of society, to which wealth has given him access, have proved in their own way as empty as the privations of his youth. Over the land at large, Wells perceives the stupid little tragedies of clipped and limited lives: 'It is matter and darkness, it is the anti-soul, it is the ruling power of this land, Stupidity.'[16] Wells does not penetrate deeply into character; rather a breezy independence of personality (not unlike

Wells's own) sweeps Kipps into life, where he must suffer the buffets of fortune. Character, formed or transformed by event, becomes the instrument through which social criticism is conveyed. And as the fiction lacks any real depth in the examination of personal behaviour, it stops short of any comprehensive analysis of the boredom and waste it portrays. Wells, for all his success in the depiction of people, is more concerned with the general contours of things than with the particular case, because he is committed to examining how the landscape as a whole may be transformed.

Tono-Bungay is conceived on a much larger scale than either *Kipps* or *Mr. Polly*. Its opening chapters (which again reflect Wells's youth, when his mother was 'in service') depict the decline of the rural squirearchy, and the traditions and beliefs which had nourished life around the large country house. There comes a time in the young Ponderevo's life when he realises that Bladesover House is not all it seems. He begins to doubt whether Mr. Bartlett, the vicar, does really know with certainty all about God; and he begins to question 'the final rightness of the gentlefolks, their primary necessity in the scheme of things'.[17] That scepticism, once awakened in Ponderevo, is to have far-reaching effects on his life because, like other men of his time, he is to find it far easier to discard beliefs than to construct them again. It is, however, also his saving virtue, for it enables him to see how the social system jostles people out of sight, to fester as they might—and expects them to be grateful for it. This is not Ponderevo's way, nor that of his uncle, under whose inventive influence he falls. Uncle George knows that it's trade which makes the world go round; and together they make the patent medicine, 'Tono-Bungay', hum. Although it's slightly injurious rubbish, it brings them 'wealth, influence, respect, the confidence of endless people'. But Ponderevo has a wider eye for the general disposition of things. In conversation with the young sculptor Ewart, he has already probed the rationale of human activity in London —but without coming to any satisfactory conclusion: ' "There must be some sense in it," I said. "We're young." ' But the failure of his marriage, in the midst of his worldly success, leaves him with a deepening awareness of the void by which he is surrounded: '. . . the real need is something that we can hold and that holds one. . . .'

He turns in the end, as many men of his time did, to science: 'In the end of this particular crisis of which I tell so badly, I idealised Science. I decided that in power and knowledge lay the salvation of my life, the secret that would fill my need.'[18] He abandons his involvement with Tono-Bungay for aeroplane experiments and engineering science. As time passes, his conviction of the need for change—change in society, and the change that can come about through the progress of scientific knowledge—becomes more acute. Scientific truth is the one reality he can discover 'in the strange disorder of existence'. His uncle, now 'apparently' hugely wealthy, has embarked upon the construction of Crest Hill house, with its miles of surrounding wall. For his nephew, it symbolises the waste and folly of our being. And with the collapse of his uncle's empire, it becomes even more a sign of the vanity and the misconception of man's endeavour: 'What a strange, melancholy emptiness of intention that stricken enterprise seemed in the evening sunlight, what vulgar magnificence and crudity and utter absurdity! It was as idiotic as the pyramids.'[19]

But young Ponderevo cannot escape the judgement upon contemporary civilisation; he too is involved in the waste. For where has his love of science led, but to the construction of destroyers?

As I turn over the big pile of manuscripts before me, certain things become clearer to me, and particularly the immense inconsequence of my experiences. It is, I see now that I have it all before me, a story of activity and urgency and sterility. I have called it *Tono-Bungay*, but I had far better have called it *Waste*.[20]

Underlying the novel is Wells's sense that the how and why of the world is an incomprehensible mystery. But happily that does not cripple his sword-arm. If the waste is obvious wherever the eye of man turns, then the job of man is to turn that waste to constructive endeavour.

The energy and resourcefulness of a Kipps or a Mr. Polly makes them good company, even if they do not take an especially optimistic view of society. But their effective high spirits were not Wells's only answer to the waste which threatened even their amiable lives. He, like Shaw, believed in the necessity for radical change: notably in *Anticipations* (1901), which he regarded as a cornerstone of his work, and *A Modern Utopia* (1905), he explored the form this should take.

In *Anticipations* Wells set out to consider the reaction of mechanical and scientific progress upon human life and thought in the new century. On the one side, he saw the deliquescence of the old social order, with its inefficient division between the rich who did nothing, and the poor who were slaves; on the other, the rapid expansion in the technology of locomotion and communication, leading to the diffusion of cities, and the creation of a new, highly specialised, scientific class. Out of this dual process he predicted the establishment of ampler and more complicated social unities, leading eventually to the establishment of one world state, at peace with itself. The arbitrary boundaries and animosities between nations would gradually give way before a larger planetary organisation. In the still secure world before the Great War he thought that the beginnings of the new world state might be created, for instance, by wealthy men living in England and America— a kind of grand new dispensation arrived at over lunch in a country-house. These new republicans would be differentiated more and more clearly 'from the shareholder, the parasitic speculator, and the wretched multitudes of the Abyss'.[21] In the end the new republic would become a world state of rational capable men, believing there to be an effect of purpose in the totality of things. This belief would form the basis of their religion.

Wells's insistence on a sense of purpose, aimed at a definite goal, and a belief in the meaningfulness of life itself, reflect the preoccupations of his time. If much in the detail of *Anticipations* now sounds absurd, its central contention of the need to overcome the inadequacies of social organisation at home, and to replace the rivalries of warring nations abroad with some organisation capable of ensuring stability and peace, has proved increasingly accurate. Wells was to return to these ideas in his later works. An ardent opponent of Marx for his emphasis upon, and incitement of, class-warfare, Wells had little taste for any system of government which made its dogma of supreme importance. Both individualism and socialism were, in the absolute, absurdities to him: 'The state is for Individuals, the law is for freedoms, the world is for experiment, experience, and change. . . .'[22] But this change needed to be in the direction of the synthesis of all cultures and policies and races into one world state, under the control of world government. The establishment of the League of Nations at the end of the Great War appeared to him a momentous opportunity to set humanity moving in this direction. Sufficiently influential in the later part of his life to gain access to Roosevelt and Stalin, he soon learnt how little they were interested in any plan to dismantle national sovereignty, or to make the League of Nations anything remotely like a prototype of world government.

Nevertheless, Wells continued to expound his beliefs and his hopes: 'I see myself in life as part of a great physical being that strains and I believe grows towards beauty, and of a great mental being that strains and I believe grows towards knowledge and power.'[23] In the end, the species was more important than the individual; though he disliked the socialism of revolt, he believed in a socialism which was 'the subordination of the will of the self-seeking individual to the idea of a racial well-being embodied in an organised state. . . .'[24] The aim of socialism was to help to create a world city of mankind—though not out of a spirit of hate: 'We have to live in a provisional state while we dream of and work for a better one. . . .'[25] Wells's tone is very close here to that of Shaw; but the way in which he sees the future is, both in shape and detail, different. Shaw was more interested in money; Wells in power.

It would be easy to dismiss much in Wells's talk about the new republic and world government as mere vapouring (just as Shaw's evolutionary philosophy is often dismissed). But that is unjust to the manner in which it emerges from his serious wrestling with the social and metaphysical problems of his time. What Wells rightly feared was that the increasing diversification and haphazard organisation of European society would cause it to dissolve into choas, unless some organising vision and system was found. Muddle—as in Forster, though in a much more public way—was the enemy.

But one cannot read far in Wells's fiction without becoming aware that what he believes to be necessary to make a better—or even viable— human future fits very uneasily both with his view of human nature and with the new dangerous potentialities of the scientific age. In *The New Machiavelli* (1911), for example, the narrator's father impresses him with a 'great ideal of order and economy which he called variously Science and Civilisation, and which, though I do not remember that he ever used that word, I suppose many people nowadays would identify with Socialism—as the Fabians expound it'.[26]

Such order, as is possible, Dick soon learns for himself, comes from the mind of man; 'otherwise natural selection, operating haphazardly, rules the universe. Order and devotion were the very essence of our socialism, and a splendid collective vigour and happiness its end.'[27] But in the contemporary world, it is easier to formulate a philosophy than to find a way of life which expresses what one believes. A fellowship is abandoned, and the narrator takes to writing: 'I had then the precise image that still serves me as symbol for all I wish to bring about, the image of an engineer building a lock in a swelling torrent—with water pressure as his only source of power. . . . Somewhere between politics and literature my grip must needs be found, but where?'[28] In Wells's fiction we hear the voice of a man appalled by 'the pitiless cruelty of a world as yet uncontrolled by any ordered will', and determined not to 'be beaten back to futility and a meaningless acquiescence in existent things. . . .' But as Dick discovers, the determination does not produce a solution, either in individual lives or in social activity. Wells describes himself accurately in this period as a 'baffled revolutionary', aware how easy it is to betray oneself in private as well as in public life.

Unlike the writers of the previous section, Wells had little talent for conveying the 'inscape' of character. He portrayed people mainly from the outside, and in social terms. But he was not unaware of the importance of the inner life. The well-being of the community depended upon the individual not being stultified; and this in turn meant a constant questioning of society's conventions and attitudes. Wells approved of an experimental attitude to life; but he also saw its dangers if the more destructive powers which man now had at his disposal were not controlled. And this involved a dilemma which Wells never resolved. He recognised the passions and pressures which made men what they were; but he also believed in a rational, ordered arrangement of human affairs, if man was not to destroy himself in the new age of scientific power and metaphysical unbelief. But the longer he lived— and especially as the result of the Second World War—the more he saw absolutely no sign of this rational society emerging. Events seemed to 'follow upon one another in an entirely untrustworthy sequence'.[29] But what brought his mind to the 'end of its tether' also highlighted how much he had been hoping for in his view of the coming world state. It involved a change in human attitudes as fundamental as Shaw's did, if creative and directed evolution were to be achieved.

He implicitly admitted this in one of his most imaginative fictions, *In the days of the comet* (1906), which also brought together his skills as a writer of fantasy and a portrayer of contemporary society. The novel envisages a Europe on the verge of a war between England and Germany. More vehemently than *Tono-Bungay*, it depicts the impoverished life of a young man without social opportunity, or education, at the start of the century. He lives in a landscape of urban squalor, where people endure a grimy and wretched existence without hope of reprieve, while the rich and well born inherit the pleasures and comforts of the earth. The young Willie Leadford dreams of a revolution which

will overthrow the existing order, and make the happiness of the few
available to the underprivileged many. His misery, and his desire for
revenge, are magnified when the girl whom he loves deserts him for
Edward Verrall, a conspicuous example of privilege in birth and education, who through his clothes and manner alone can humiliate Willie
whenever he chooses. Armed with a revolver, Willie sets out to track
down the lovers on their honeymoon. This story of personal vendetta
is set against the mounting tension of a miners' strike, and the escala-
tion of conflict between England and Germany. As Willie catches up
with the lovers, the battleships off the coast start to fire; and violence
looks as though it will once more destroy the frail fabric of order.

But while human beings are preoccupied by conflict, a mysterious
comet has been approaching the earth; and, as it draws near, it encompasses human life in a thick green vapour. Men lose consciousness;
and when they awake, they have been transformed. In the place of the
old irrational hatred and hostility, they feel goodwill towards their
fellow men. In the new world-state love and peace prevail. Even the
possessive love which compelled Willie to hate Edward has given way
to an acceptance that Nettie can love them each in her own way. The
destructive passions have been destroyed and turned into acceptance
and concord. Wells succeeds in conveying the reality of this transformed
world—both because it is presented as the result of a mysterious occurrence, which no one is capable of resisting, and because the wonder of it
does not immediately remove the problems. Willie has still to struggle
to see the changed relationships between himself and Edward, even
though the hatred has disappeared. Also change has not meant oblivion.
Willie remembers the former world in its ugliness and hopelessness;
and this memory makes the more plausible his new-found joy and
elation. He can now walk in the world as a beautiful place.

In the days of the comet is a scientist's version of The Tempest; and like
The Tempest it suggests how men might be if they passed through 'a
sea-change'. When Wells argued in his essays the need for a world state,
he did not succeed in making it seem likely, however strong the arguments in its favour were—not least because he did not consider how
nations were to be persuaded to give up a large part of their sovereignty,
or how the power of the world government was to be controlled, once
established. But here he does not strain the reader's credulity, because
the change in human nature occurs as the result of a mysterious planetary
influence at a moment when man would otherwise appear to be

engineering his own demise. The change involves the victory of the higher human attributes over the baser; and though Wells was by no means sure that this would occur, he consistently tried to imagine how it might come about, because he saw all too clearly the consequences of failure. His restless and inventive intellect was intent upon weighing up the human race's chance of survival with any decency, in an age of unparalleled power, and urging those courses which seemed to him to offer the largest hope.

Wells proved no more capable than Shaw or Péguy of persuading society of the truth of what he said. As he grew older, his dreams of the advancement of human society receded; and like them he was left with the words which express the hope, but not the means of realisation. In the works of all three, the inadequacies and menace of the modern world transformed the 'why' of the sceptic into the 'why not' of the visionary. Good reason exists for being suspicious of utopianism or impractical idealism. But in their individual ways they direct our attention to what should not be accepted in the human condition, and to the hope of advance in the future. In doing this they celebrate the potentiality of the common life we share, whether or not their particular visions are fulfilled; and whether or not we believe their particular solutions to be correct. When men cease to have the conviction of Péguy, Shaw and Wells that individual life without hope of leaving the world a better place would be intolerable, the world and its art will be the poorer.

RICHARD WAGNER: AN AFTERWORD

Noch losch das Licht nicht aus
noch ward's nich Nacht in Haus. . . .
(The light is still not quenched; not yet is it dark in the house. . . .)
Tristan und Isolde, Act Two

The art of literature is descriptive and particular. In reading a writer's works we see what he says; and we judge the value of what has been said through an appreciation of its form. Music without words is not descriptive, but expressive. Unless the composer tells us the source of his music, we can never know what that was—or indeed if it had any source other than a musical idea. In opera the words give assistance; and in Wagner's operas, in particular, the words give direction and precision to the symphonic flow of the music. They relate the stories out of which the music's expressive power grows; they make us aware of the conflict of character, and finally they point to the dramatic emotion which the music simultaneously expresses in its own pure form. Even in Wagner's operas the precise nature of the musical effect—its meaning—remains unknowable. Its value resides in what at some level it does for us, and gives to us.

Hatred and idolatry of Wagner are equally common, and equally ill-founded. Hatred of Wagner because of his association with the Nazis deflects attention from the subject of his music: no work says more clearly than *The Ring* that 'power tends to corrupt and absolute power corrupts absolutely.' Idolatry of Wagner often fails to consider the manner in which his music, as well as his drama, challenges our desire to think well of ourselves. Exploring the dark recesses and impulses of human consciousness, the music reminds us of much that is repugnant about us. In particular the experience of our capacity to hate becomes a necessary part of the journey towards the conclusions the music finally reaches. Wagner wrestled with the nature of the human psyche, and discovered that dark as the powers were within it, they were not stronger than the forces of light; but he did not do so without compelling us to hear and see how our involvement with the world was so nearly catastrophic. To submit to the music is neither an easy nor palatable experience. In the early works, *Tannhäuser* and *Lohengrin*, much in the Christian framework of the libretto gave the completed work a nineteenth-century accent; but in *The Ring* and *Tristan*, where he used a more primitive mythology, he impelled both music and drama towards the anxiety and self-doubt of the twentieth century.

The interpretation of Wagner's *Ring* has ranged from Shaw's analysis of it as a socialist manifesto to Robert Donington's profound study of its relation to the psychological viewpoint of Jung. Like any great work of art, its chameleon form corresponds both to the perceptions of depth psychology and to the human world which we recognise as external observers. As music and mythology, its massive architecture (itself a supreme act of courage over twenty years of creative labour without prospect of production) is constructed from foundations as deep as Nibelheim, where the mists of the unconscious enshroud those instincts which make us both slaves and aggressors. Alberich and Hagen, as characters and musical identities, project what is hateful and dark in human personality, and transform the compromises and weaknesses of the Gods into the instruments of destruction and catastrophe. The struggle for power has no end. As one mortal triumphs and another falls, the cycle of the Ring is completed, giving way to another where the same struggle and impulses will manifest themselves yet again. As in the grove at Nemi, the King who slew his predecessor waits for the next King who will inevitably slay him. The struggle for power is implicit too in the struggle between generations: son succeeds father, Siegfried replaces Wotan: not to succeed any better in the unequal chances of life, but to fall victim too in his own way and place.

Here we are in a world darker than the Shakespearean histories where the wars of succession are themselves conceived in terms of Christian and humanist thought, and men's consciences still inform them where right action lies, even if they deliberately choose to reject it. Alberich has no conscience: he sees the world without moral sanctions. What he desires is justified by his desire, and his determination to satisfy his lusts by cunning. Alberich is unthinking impulse, the will to whatever he wants; Hagen, his son, embodies that impulse in a human world, willing to murder those like Gunther who harbour him, and to encourage those like Gutrune in schemes which further his purpose, without reference to the damage he does. Those who do not suspect the depths of possible evil in man will inevitably fall victim to him. He has the advantage of purposiveness, absolute in its intentions. Alberich and Hagen exist in the forefront of our attention; the progress of the world moves more according to the direction of their will than to that of any other force. And Wagner fills his music with loathing for the attitudes and impulses they embody.

The middle-ground of the action is taken up with compromised beings—more like ourselves as we normally appear—confused in their judgements and uncertain in their actions. In this territory Wagner's depiction of human types is various. At one extreme, Mime, capable of nurturing the foundling Siegfried, is equally capable of killing him when it serves the purpose of his cupidity. Mime is the servant and forger of material wealth, undirected by any deep human principle, unthinking, plaintive—the man who does not know what it means to take responsibility for his life. At the opposite extreme, Wotan, deeply human, exercises his authority without fully realising the responsibility it involves. He too becomes the slave of the image of his own material splendour, willing to sacrifice Freia to pay for Valhalla, and then to rob Nibelheim in the attempt to rescind his contract. The upholder of laws and institutions, Wotan is nonetheless willing to forget them when they offend his personal affections: himself a lawbreaker, he punishes those like Brunnhilde who break his laws. But Wotan, in spite of his irresponsibility and confusion, is god-like in other ways: he knows that not only his own will matters; he listens to Loge, Fricka and Erda; he uses his authority to prevent unnecessary strife, and he loves the disobedient Brunnhilde. His farewell to her conveys not merely the feeling of the moment, but the knowledge that he is losing a relationship which cannot be replaced. All that feeling remains with him too when, as the Wanderer in *Siegfried*, he recalls her sleeping form; and in Waltraute's account of him powerless within Valahalla. Between Mime's shallowness and Wotan's compromised divinity, Wagner depicts others, neither wholly good, nor wholly bad—Hunding, Gunther, Gutrune, Fricka—men and Gods who defend their rights, and, in defending them, are involved in the strife of the world. Such strife too is not only of individual contriving, but the outcome of forces—like the Rhinemaidens and Norns—which symbolise the immersion of humanity in the mystery of things.

The foreground and middle-ground of *The Ring*, in its depiction of dark impulses, ill will, confusion, arbitrariness and struggle, amounts to a harsh and fierce account of the universe; but the background adds a quite different dimension, not altogether susceptible of interpretation, because finally expressing itself in music alone. But it indicates a transcendent reality springing out of human love, both a part of it, and greater than it too.

The depiction of love in *The Ring* takes many forms: love as loyalty to, and affection for, Freia; love as ecstatic union between Siegmund and Siegelinde; as deep paternal affection between Wotan and Brunnhilde, and as an eternal bond between Brunnhilde and Siegfried. Their love differs from that between Siegmund and Siegelinde, which contains all the wonder of a sudden discovery. Brunnhilde and Siegfried's has neither beginning nor end:

> Ewig war ich,
> ewig bin ich
> ewig in süss
> sehnender Wonne,
> doch ewig zu deinem Heil:[1]

So begins the Siegfried idyll; and Siegfried in dying reasserts its truth:

> Er küsst dich wach
> und aber der Braut
> bricht er die Bande
> da licht ihm Brunnhildes Lust!
> Ach! Dieses Auge,
> ewig nun offen![2]

This love between Brunnhilde and Siegfried exists first on a human plane—it is as Siegfried's wife that Brunnhilde, riding into the flames, greets him. But here the music takes over. It is not only the love of two people which is conveyed to us; but the power of love to overcome the

---

[1] I always was
I always am
always lapped in sweet
longing bliss
always caring for your good.

[2] He kissed you awake
and when the bride's
bonds were broken,
Brunnhilde's joy smiled on him.
Ah, those eyes
opened for ever.

struggle for power, to create for itself a reality that transcends actualities —complete, absolute and will-less. With no desire for anything other than itself it is redeemed from the world of desire for domination, of malice and compromise in which human beings live. No opera (and few works of art in general) says more clearly than *The Ring* that material splendour is ephemeral; and although *The Ring* paints that splendour in music and action, it simultaneously presents it as cursed and part of power's illusion. But in concentrating so much of its attention on the normal world in all its darkness, it discovers a reality capable of opposing and triumphing over it. *The Ring* does not purge us of our emotions in the classical sense; it makes us more aware of their nature.

In its preoccupation with conflict, and the desire for domination as man's primary psychological drive, *The Ring* does not have much to say about friendship. But *Tristan and Isolde* combines a view of friendship with an even more extreme and absolute statement of Wagner's view of love. In relation to the second, Act Two of *Tristan* must be counted among the most remarkable achievements of western European art.

In the final scene of *Tristan*, King Mark refers to him as his 'treulos treuster Freund'.* In everything which Tristan has done, except in his love for Isolde, he has served his King with the utmost loyalty; Mark regards him as the embodiment of honour and virtue; and his grief springs not from the lovers' infidelity, but from the disloyalty where he had trusted long and well. It is neither with Mark's approval, nor at his instigation that the jealous Melot strikes Tristan down. Like Hagen, Melot uses a pretended loyalty to work out his own desire for revenge; and like Hagen he pays for it with his life. In the Wagnerian world those whose motivation is destructive are never shown as triumphant. Aware to an intense degree of the evil of which man is capable, Wagner nonetheless sees good as the dominant force. When the opera ends, Mark is left grieving for his dead friend, not angry for the dishonour done him. He has pursued the lovers to Careol, not to part them, but to wed them—only to find that frenzy and malevolence have forestalled him. Mark, in his generosity, stands for the highest ideal of friendship: unpossessive and unembittered, except by the sorrow of things. He brings to the human world a large-mindedness incapable of controlling the forces of destruction, but remaining himself undestroyed

* Faithless, yet most faithful friend.

because of it. Wagner leaves no doubt by the music he writes for Mark, about the value which he attaches to such steadfastness. But in a world of passions as implacable as those of *The Ring* and *Tristan* it must stand as a virtue in reserve against any wholly depressing account of things, not as a solution. And *Tristan*, like *The Ring*, does contain a solution of its own kind.

The love-duet between Tristan and Isolde in Act Two expresses through music and words the desire for an absolute union. It makes use of the death-wish to convey the desire for love's night not to end. But it also celebrates night as the proper sphere of love, in contrast to daylight which contains the 'lies' of honour and fame, power and profit. The will, operating in day towards empty ambitions and goals, is replaced in the night by the stasis of love, no longer subject to change, or the vicissitudes which desire brings about. All which normally attracts has been scattered like barren dust in the sun; and the night which brings death to such attractions allows the harmony of freedom from will to take their place. Both Tristan and Isolde may sing together:

> selbst bin ich dann die Welt. . . .*

Joined together in one consciousness, they are freed from fear and grief. When finally Mark and Melot break in on the lovers they are destroying this state of stillness, and bringing them back to the world where they will be forced once more to participate in the conflict of human wills and desires. When they celebrate night and death, they do not do so as a quiescence but as an alternative to the world as normally experienced. Like mystical experience the time allowed to their love is brief, compared to the extent of life which surrounds it. In the 'Liebestod' Wagner conveys its continuing existence; but not so much in terms of particular lovers as of a view of things they have allowed us to share. Isolde's final words express a much more important idea than the desire for the end of physical life; they express a longing for unconsciousness to those desires which corrupt and destroy human life, and reduce the possibility of love such as theirs to a minimum. The opera celebrates the love that exists beyond such desires, itself the means through which the anguish and destructiveness of the world are overcome.

Wagner in his music expresses states of being which words cannot easily define, and towards which they only act as pointers. Beyond

* I myself am the world.

Wagner's music there lies the doctrine of grace, and the virtue of humility. Wagner knew little enough about either. His world, for all its use of mystical elements, is confined within the human consciousness; its healing is not that of the Holy Spirit but of depth psychology and the integration of the self. It is the consciousness of man that he celebrates in its weakness and potentiality, expressed through the darkness and beauty of music.

Wagner encompasses in *The Ring* the three main themes of this book: the courage and forbearance of man in the face of fate, the necessity for self-discovery if the individual is to be fulfilled, and the faith that makes men strive in the belief that world can be made better than it presently is. His music-dramas are profound both as political and personal truth. As a bond between them stands the massive conviction in art itself, transcending all categories of thought, and expressing in the completed idea an image of absolute truth.

CONCLUSION

The important writers of the late nineteenth century were all men who knew that the age in which they lived offered no easy solution to the problem of belief. Agnosticism had already begun to leave in its wake a void which could neither be ignored, nor easily filled. At the same time new knowledge about the universe was establishing a view of things in which reality appeared bleaker than had been previously recognised. Acts of imagination could still transform the landscape, distract, provide forms of escape; but if they were to be significant they had to represent the modified world in which people were living. There is a place—and a very important place—for the art that is just entertainment, which makes us laugh, feel more lively, turns our minds from less endurable problems, and sends us back to them more able to cope. Relief is an important attribute of human life at many levels; and those who divert or entertain are rightly valued for what they contribute. But the great artist does something of a different kind. He sees all that is dark in reality; but by the power and creativeness of his imagination he enables us to see through that reality to an order in which there is an affirmation, and a kind of rejoicing. As the world becomes darker (or appears to do so) through the accumulation of knowledge, and the tragic inability of human beings to restrain their own destructiveness, such an act becomes harder to achieve. It is not to diminish Beethoven, but to state a fact about the origin of his art, to say that the wonder and splendours of his music belong to an age when the romantic artist was regarded as visionary and prophet, gifted with special powers for perceiving beauty and truth. The artist of the late nineteenth century no longer possessed the authority, or the advantage, of this special position. An artist's work is his response to the world as he sees it; but it also has to be a response which other people can share: his work belongs to his time. The art of assertion, as practised frequently by the mid-Victorians, could not survive in a more sceptical and questioning age. But no great art can ever emerge from scepticism only—not even satire. In the late nineteenth century the task of writers was perhaps easier than it became for those writing after the First World War, and easier for them than it was after the Second. The course of human history has made it difficult, for reasons which reflect the secularisation of the European mind, and the appalling disasters we bring on ourselves (or fail to prevent), to believe that life is a good, or that human beings are in a better state than the dinosaurs at the start of the age of great dying. It is tempting to believe we are doomed; and some regard this as the only possible truth about us. To deny it—to look at all the evidence and say that one cannot see how it might be so—requires an act of faith: an act of faith in the goodness and purposiveness of human life. The facts do not bring one to such a position; but the value of facts can be overrated. To a scientist, they appear only as degrees of probability; to a non-scientist, what he thinks he knows, as opposed to what he knows he does not know. In this area of darkness where the value of facts comes to an end, the artist has room to work.

When we look back to the artists of the late nineteenth century— whether to Hardy or Shaw or Ibsen or Chekov or Wagner—we find that the world of their imagination transforms the facts as others might, and did, see them. It injects values into a system which might otherwise seem valueless. It provides grounds for supposing that cruel as life is, it contains grounds for rejoicing; that bad as things are they may be improved; and though all men must die, the future may be brighter and better for those who follow after us. In art such beliefs do not come from a conscious act of mind, but from something within the artist to which he can give expression, and which does not in a special sense belong to him. It belongs to his common humanity, which he expresses to a higher degree through his art, articulating and confirming what we only half knew.

The perspectives which are to be discovered in these acts of imagination—ranging from the investigation of the darker areas of the human psyche to the politics of the community—share one common value: that of not trivialising human existence. To immerse oneself in them is never to be left with the feeling that, if this is what we are like, and these are our preoccupations, then the process itself is unimportant. If we imagine these writers brought together in all their differences of temperament and nationality, a 'great consult' between them would reveal the measure of their commitment to humanity, and the values involved in the process of being alive. In our contemporary concern with writing well, and with being wholly honest about ourselves and our impulses, it is sometimes easy to forget that the measure of achievement does lie in a comparison with the great imaginative thinkers of the past and with the comprehensiveness of their understanding. No one could come from a reading of Dante, Shakespeare, Milton or Pascal without perceiving the splendours and abysses of human existence. The writers of the end of the last century, in their particular and diverse forms of mastery, begin to reflect the patterns of the modern world; and to insist upon the challenges—personal and social— which characterise our own time. Their awareness of an increasingly sceptical, materialistic and scientific society did not, however, deter them from the quest to reaffirm values in a new and increasingly perplexing context; though the quest took them, as we have seen, along very different roads.

Those who belong more completely to the twentieth century— notably W. B. Yeats, T. S. Eliot and W. H. Auden—fought the battle in worsened circumstances, but with no less triumphant results. Eliot's way was a way of detachment, that gave him the strength to face the dead distractions, torpidity and decay which had begun to characterise a civilisation on the wane: personal, mystic, unattached to material values, asserting repeatedly the existence of a still point in the turning world. Auden's victory was larger, more generous, more accepting and involved: a difference of personality as well as of artistic vision. His basic belief that life was a good and was to be celebrated survived the horrors of the Second World War. His dedication to his art meant a dedication to 'teaching the free man how to praise'. And his praise for what is good, observed through his great learning and catholicity of taste, remains the highest legacy of his art. After Eliot and Auden, only Samuel Beckett achieves something comparable, and in a diminishing way; not that his art is getting slighter, but that apparently his ability to rejoice in the 'beauty of the way and the goodness of the travellers' is growing less. As T. S. Eliot warned, it is becoming harder to believe anything as the twentieth century progresses. But that is still the challenge of art: the only challenge which separates it from personal allegory or dementia, posing as art; and there are plenty of both. The power to celebrate and rejoice stands also as the reward of victory in that struggle.

NOTES

Introduction (*between pages 13 and 17*)

1. Paul Valéry, 'La Crise de l'Esprit', *Oeuvres*, I, Bibliothèque de la Pléiade, Paris, 1957, p. 991.
2. Aldous Huxley, *Crome Yellow*, Collected Edition, London, 1963, p. 185.
3. W. H. Auden, 'The Cave of Making', *About the House*, London, 1966, p. 19.
4. W. de la Mare, 'Rupert Brooke and the Intellectual Imagination', London, 1919, p. 21.
5. T. S. Eliot, 'A Note on Poetry and Belief', *The Enemy*, January 1927, p. 16.
6. W. H. Auden, 'Mimesis and Allegory', *English Institute Annual*, 1940, p. 19.

Chapter 1 'The backcloth changes . . .' (*between pages 21 and 33*)

1. Isaac Newton, *Principia Mathematica*, University of Columbia, 1960, pp. 544 and 546.
2. Thomas Sprat, *History of the Royal Society*, London, 1667, p. 82.
3. John Ray, *The Wisdom of God*, London, 1692, A5v.
4. *Ibid.*, Pt. II, p. 15.
5. Thomas Malthus, *Essay on the Principle of Population*, London, 1803, p. 2.
6. *Ibid.*, p. 350.
7. *Ibid.*, pp. 502–3.
8. W. Paley, *Natural Theology*, London, 1803, p. 490.
9. C. Darwin, *On the Origin of Species*, 1872, p. 163.
10. John Milton, *Paradise Lost*, Bk. VII, ll. 452–6, London, 1958, p. 159.
11. James Hutton, *Theory of the Earth*, London, 1795, Vol. I, p. 20.
12. *Ibid.*, Vol. II, p. 562.
13. *Ibid.*, Vol. I, p. 200.
14. Charles Lyell, *Principles of Geology*, London, 1830, Vol. I, p. 65.
15. *Ibid.*, 1833, Vol. III, pp. 384–5.
16. Charles Darwin, *On the Origin of Species*, London, 1859, Vol. I, p. 282.
17. *Ibid.*, Vol. I, p. 83.
18. Amy Cruse, *The Victorians and their Books*, London, 1939, p. 397.
19. P. du Chaillu, *Explorations and Adventures in Equatorial Africa*, London, 1861, p. 71.
20. Oscar Wilde, 'The Critic as Artist', *Works*, edited by G. F. Maine, London, 1954, p. 997.
21. A. O. J. Cockshut, *Anglican Attitudes*, London, 1959, p. 87.
22. Samuel Johnson, *The Rambler*, 21 December 1761.

23. Wyndham Lewis, *Time and Western Man*, London, 1927, p. 366.
24. Joseph Conrad, *Nostromo*, 1904, Collected Edition, London, 1974, p. 498.
25. T. S. Eliot, 'The Dry Salvages', *Collected Poems*, 1909–62, London, 1963, p. 208.

Chapter 2   The case of Tolstoy (*between pages 34 and 43*)

1. Leo Tolstoy, *A Confession*, translated by Aylmer Maude, World's Classics, London, 1961, p. 8.
2. *Ibid.*, p. 13.
3. *Ibid.*, p. 42.
4. *Ibid.*, p. 53.
5. *On Life*, translated by Aylmer Maude, World's Classics, London, 1934, p. 29.
6. *Ibid.*, p. 128.
7. *What is Art?*, translated by Aylmer Maude, World's Classics, London, 1962, p. 50.
8. *The Death of Ivan Ilych*, translated by Louise and Aylmer Maude, World's Classics, London, 1959, p. 1.
9. *Ibid.*, p. 3.
10. *Ibid.*, p. 25.
11. *The Kreutzer Sonata*, translated by Aylmer Maude, World's Classics, London, 1960, p. 204.
12. *Ibid.*, p. 209.
13. *Resurrection*, translated by Rosemary Edmonds, Penguin Classics, Harmondsworth, 1966, p. 74.
14. *Ibid.*, p. 335.
15. *Ibid.*, p. 407.
16. *The Law of Love, and the Law of Violence*, translated by Mary Tolstoy, London, 1970, p. 8.

Chapter 3   Thomas Hardy (*between pages 47 and 60*)

(All page references to the New Wessex edition.)
1. Thomas Hardy, *A Pair of Blue Eyes*, p. 222.
2. *The Woodlanders*, p. 82.
3. *The Mayor of Casterbridge*, p. 320.
4. *The Return of the Native*, p. 205.
5. *The Mayor of Casterbridge*, p. 160.
6. *Tess of the D'Urbervilles*, p. 309.
7. *Far from the Madding Crowd*, p. 278.
8. *Ibid.*, p. 279.
9. *Ibid.*, p. 280.
10. *Ibid.*, p. 395.
11. *The Return of the Native*, p. 34.
12. *Ibid.*, p. 35.
13. *Ibid.*, p. 45.
14. *Ibid.*, p. 156.
15. *Ibid.*, p. 353.

16. *Ibid.*, p. 376.
17. *The Woodlanders*, p. 341.
18. *Ibid.*, p. 316.
19. *Ibid.*, p. 375.
20. *Tess of the D'Urbervilles*, p. 28.
21. *Ibid.*, p. 39.
22. *Ibid.*, p. 114.
23. *Ibid.*, p. 122.
24. *Ibid.*, p. 418.
25. *Ibid.*, p. 403.
26. *Ibid.*, p. 363.
27. *Ibid.*, p. 416.
28. *Jude the Obscure*, p. 346.
29. *The Mayor of Casterbridge*, p. 314.
30. *Complete Poems*, p. 150.
31. *Ibid.*, p. 475.

Chapter 4 Joseph Conrad (*between pages 61 and 71*)

1. Joseph Conrad, *Almayer's Folly*, Collected Edition, London, 1947, p. 71.
2. *Ibid.*, p. 192.
3. *The Heart of Darkness*, Collected Edition, 1967, p. 62.
4. *Ibid.*, pp. 151–2.
5. *Lord Jim*, Collected Edition, 1974, p. 89.
6. *Nostromo*, Collected Edition, 1974, p. 566.
7. *Ibid.*, p. 84.
8. *Ibid.*, p. 521.
9. *Ibid.*, p. 497.
10. *Victory*, Collected Edition, 1967, p. v.
11. *Ibid.*, p. 228.
12. *Ibid.*, pp. 410–11.
13. *Ibid.*, p. 407.
14. *Ibid.*, p. 410.
15. Bertrand Russell, 'A Free Man's Worship', *Mysticism and Logic*, London, 1918, p. 54.

Chapter 5 Thomas Mann (*between pages 72 and 87*)

1. Thomas Mann, *Letters*, Vol. I, 1889–1942, London, 1970, p. 50.
2. *Ibid.*, p. 48.
3. Thomas Mann: *Stories of a Lifetime*, Vol. I, London, 1961, p. 7.
4. *Ibid.*, p. 9.
5. *Ibid.*, p. 26.
6. *Ibid.*, pp. 27–8.
7. *Ibid.*, p. 67.
8. *Ibid.*, p. 67.
9. *Ibid.*, p. 92.
10. *Ibid.*, p. 92.

11. *Letters, op. cit.,* p. 48.
12. Quoted in T. J. Reed, *The Uses of Tradition,* Oxford, 1974, p. 71.
13. *Buddenbrooks,* translated by H. T. Lowe-Porter, Penguin Modern Classics, Harmondsworth, 1975, p. 503.
14. *Ibid.,* p. 503.
15. *Ibid.,* p. 364.
16. *Ibid.,* p. 518.
17. *Ibid.,* p. 586.
18. *Stories of a Lifetime,* Vol. I, pp. 331–2.
19. *Ibid.,* p. 141.
20. *Ibid.,* p. 173.
21. *Ibid.,* p. 205.
22. *Letters, op. cit.,* p. 76.
23. *Stories of a Lifetime,* Vol. II, p. 13.
24. *Ibid.,* p. 46.
25. *Ibid.,* p. 54.
26. *Ibid.,* p. 52.
27. *Ibid.,* p. 44.
28. *Ibid.,* p. 71.
29. *Ibid.,* p. 14.

Chapter 6   Henrik Ibsen (*between pages 91 and 109*)

1. Oscar Wilde, *Works,* London, 1954, p. 867.
2. *The Soul of Man under Socialism, Works,* p. 1040.
3. *Dorian Gray, Works,* p. 29.
4. *Ibid.,* p. 140.
5. *De Profundis, Works,* p. 857.
6. *Ibid.,* p. 858.
7. *Ibid.,* p. 858.
8. *Ibid.,* p. 859.
9. *Ibid.,* p. 887.
10. August Strindberg, *The Road to Damascus,* translated by Graham Rowson, London, 1958, p. 150.
11. *Twelve Plays of Strindberg,* translated by Elizabeth Sprigge, London, 1962, p. 689.
12. *The Road to Damascus,* p. 195.
13. *Ibid.,* p. 267.
14. Henrik Ibsen, *An Enemy of the People,* translated by Michael Meyer, London, 1963, p. 118.
15. Quoted by Michael Meyer in *Henrik Ibsen, the farewell to poetry, 1864–1882,* London, 1971, p. 144.
16. *Brand,* translated by Michael Meyer, London, 1967, p. 112.
17. *Peer Gynt,* translated by Norman Ginsbury, 1960, p. 167.
18. T. J. Reed, *The Uses of Tradition,* Oxford, 1974, p. 71.
19. *When We Dead Awaken,* translated by Michael Meyer, London, 1960, p. 69.

Chapter 7 Anton Chekov (*between pages 110 and 122*)

1. Quoted by Ernest Simmons in *Chekov, A Biography*, London, 1963, p. 495.
2. *Ibid.*, p. 581.
3. Chekov, *Plays*, translated by Elisaveta Fen, Penguin Classics, Harmondsworth, 1959, *The Cherry Orchard*, Act II, p. 363.
4. *Ibid.*, pp. 363–4.
5. Simmons, *op. cit.*, p. 17.
6. *Ibid.*, p. 581.
7. *Lady with Lapdog, and other stories*, translated by David Magarshack, Penguin Classics, Harmondsworth, 1964, *Ward Number Six*, p. 143.
8. *Ibid.*, p. 143.
9. *Ibid.*, p. 175.
10. The Oxford Chekov, Vol. 6, *Stories 1892–93*, translated by Ronald Hingley, London, 1971, *Neighbours*, p. 104.
11. *Ibid.*, p. 115.
12. *Ibid.*, p. 117.
13. *The Darling*, translated by David Magarshack, *op. cit.* (note 7), p. 255.
14. *Ibid.*, p. 260.
15. *Ibid.*, p. 263.
16. *Ionych, op. cit.* (note 7), p. 243.
17. *Ibid.*, p. 250.
18. *The House with an Attic, op. cit.* (note 7), p. 228.
19. *Plays, op. cit., The Seagull*, Act IV, p. 181.
20. *Plays, Uncle Vania*, Act I, p. 195.
21. *Ibid.*, Act II, p. 205.
22. *Ibid.*, Act II, p. 211.
23. *Ibid.*, Act IV, p. 244.
24. *Ibid.*, Act IV, p. 245.
25. *Plays, Three Sisters*, Act IV, p. 318.
26. *Ibid.*, Act I, p. 266.
27. *Ibid.*, Act IV, p. 329.
28. *Ibid.*, Act II, p. 281.
29. *Ibid.*, p. 278.
30. *Ibid.*, p. 293.
31. *Ibid.*, Act III, p. 304.
32. *Plays, The Cherry Orchard*, Act II, p. 354.
33. *Ibid.*, p. 357.
34. *Ibid.*, p. 357.
35. *Ibid.*, p. 359.
36. *Ibid.*, pp. 367–8.
37. *Ibid.*, Act I, p. 333.

Chapter 8 E. M. Forster (*between pages 123 and 137*)

1. P. N. Furbank, *E. M. Forster, a Life*, Vol. I, 1879–1914, London, 1977, p. 62.
2. E. M. Forster, *Where Angels Fear to Tread*, Penguin Modern Classics, Harmondsworth, 1959, pp. 41–2.

3. *Ibid.*, p. 154.
4. *Ibid.*, p. 160.
5. *The Longest Journey*, Penguin Modern Classics, Harmondsworth, 1960, p. 23.
6. *Ibid.*, p. 66.
7. *Ibid.*, p. 86.
8. *Ibid.*, p. 142.
9. *Ibid.*, p. 146.
10. *Ibid.*, p. 180.
11. *A Room with a View*, Penguin Modern Classics, Harmondsworth, 1955, p. 214.
12. *Ibid.*, p. 256.
13. *Ibid.*, p. 85.
14. *Ibid.*, p. 163.
15. *Ibid.*, p. 198.
16. *Ibid.*, p. 214.
17. *Ibid.*, p. 250.
18. *Howards End*, Penguin Modern Classics, Harmondsworth, 1977, p. 300.
19. *Ibid.*, p. 36.
20. *Ibid.*, p. 253.
21. *Ibid.*, p. 325.
22. *A Passage to India*, Penguin Modern Classics, Harmondsworth, 1969, p. 299.

Chapter 9 Charles Péguy (*between pages 141 and 152*)

1. Maurice Maeterlinck, *Treasury of the Humble*, translated by Alfred Sutro, London, 1901, p. 30.
2. Charles Péguy, *Oeuvres Poétiques Complètes*, Bibliothèque de la Pléiade, Paris, 1960, p. 328.
3. *Ibid.*, p. 23.
4. *Ibid.*, p. 46.
5. *Ibid.*, p. 159.
6. *Ibid.*, p. 92.
7. *Ibid.*, p. 216.
8. *Ibid.*, p. 661.

Chapter 10 George Bernard Shaw (*between pages 153 and 164*)

1. Bertrand Russell, *Autobiography*, 1872–1914, I, London, 1967, p. 53.
2. George Bernard Shaw, *Complete Plays*, London. 1965, p. 1167.
3. *Ibid.*, p. 92.
4. *Ibid.*, pp. 250–1.
5. *Ibid.*, p. 292.
6. *Ibid.*, p. 292.
7. *Ibid.*, p. 291.
8. *Ibid.*, p. 499.
9. *Ibid.*, p. 499.
10. *Ibid.*, p. 484.
11. *Ibid.*, p. 485.

12. *Ibid.*, p. 499.
13. *Ibid.*, p. 502.
14. *Ibid.*, p. 503.
15. *Ibid.*, pp. 385–6.
16. *Ibid.*, p. 388.
17. *Ibid.*, p. 962.
18. *Ibid.*, p. 1011.
19. *Ibid.*, p. 292.

Chapter 11 H. G. Wells (*between pages 165 and 179*)

1. H. G. Wells, *Experiment in Autobiography* (2 Vols.), London, 1934, II, p. 541.
2. *Ibid.*, I, p. 82.
3. *Ibid.*, I, p. 161.
4. *Ibid.*, II, p. 643.
5. *A Modern Utopia*, Atlantic Edition of the *Works* of H. G. Wells (20 Vols.), London, 1924, Vol. IX, p. 7.
6. *The Time Machine*, Atlantic Edition, Vol. I, p. 3.
7. *The Island of Doctor Moreau*, Atlantic Edition, Vol. II, p. 94.
8. *Ibid.*, p. 170.
9. *The Invisible Man*, Atlantic Edition, Vol. III, p. 403.
10. *Ibid.*, p. 201.
11. *The War of the Worlds*, Atlantic Edition, Vol. III, p. 403.
12. *Ibid.*, p. 449.
13. *The History of Mr. Polly*, Atlantic Edition, Vol. XVII, p. 153.
14. *Ibid.*, p. 164.
15. *Ibid.*, p. 212.
16. *Kipps*, Atlantic Edition, Vol. VIII, p. 415.
17. *Tono-Bungay*, Atlantic Edition, Vol. XII, p. 11.
18. *Ibid.*, p. 271.
19. *Ibid.*, p. 472.
20. *Ibid.*, p. 519.
21. *Anticipations*, Atlantic Edition, Vol. IX, p. 240.
22. *A Modern Utopia, op. cit.*, p. 82.
23. *First and Last Things*, London, 1929, p. 60.
24. *Ibid.*, pp. 78–9.
25. *Ibid.*, p. 97.
26. *The New Machiavelli*, Atlantic Edition, Vol. XIV, p. 37.
27. *Ibid.*, pp. 154–5.
28. *Ibid.*, p. 216.
29. *Mind at the end of its tether*, London, 1945, p. 6.

Richard Wagner: an afterword (*between pages 180 and 186*)
1. *Siegfried*, Act III.
2. *Götterdämmerung*, Act III.
   Translations are by William Mann, 1964.

INDEX OF AUTHORS AND WORKS